RENTAL PROPERTY AND MINIMALIST BUDGET

2-in-1 Book

Generate Massive Passive Income with Rental Properties and Flipping Houses + Smart Money Management Strategies to Budget Your Money Effectively

REAL ESTATE INVESTING: RENTAL PROPERTY

Discover How To Generate Massive Passive Income With Rental Properties, Flipping Houses, Commercial & Residential Real Estate, Even With No Money Down

Table of Contents

Introduction

Does your uncle rent out his second apartment for $1500 a month and you want in on the action? Living the life of a landlord is a dream. Consider the possibilities: If you could rent 10 apartments for $1500 a month each, you could easily add $15,000 in passive income to your wallet every month for the rest of your life. Have you ever rented from a landlord who owns 5, 10 or maybe 50 condos, and makes a full-time living simply by renting properties? Do you ever wonder how they got there and got funding? In most cases, landlords didn't inherit their properties. They started out with a few acquisitions and expanded their ownership to numerous properties.

Do you want to get started in real estate but don't know where to find funding? There are ways to buy rental properties without being a millionaire. This book will teach you all the secrets you want to know about rental properties. If you have little or no money at all and don't know where to start, we'll teach you how to finance your rental properties without a significant investment. Yes, it's possible - and yes there are ways to secure hundreds of thousands of dollars without using your mom's house as collateral. We'll give you insight into the landlord mindset: You will learn how to finance properties with little to no initial investment and we'll tell you how to find tenants and enjoy a stress-free lifestyle for the rest of your life.

Revelation #1: Rental Properties Are Stable Income.

Renting is the easiest form of real estate investment, a lot easier than flipping properties full time. To become a landlord, you merely have to acquire a property and put it on the market. You'll be able to find tenants for even the worst, most run-down properties. Compare that to flipping, where the flipper has to put down a payment for a property, repair structural damage, refurbish the interior, and wait an average of six months while a house that might not sell at all sits on the market.

A landlord could technically purchase a property and rent it out the next day. So, you tell me which is easier, renting or flipping? The hard part of rental income is making a long-term profit. It's your job to learn how to finance multiple properties at once to be able to sustain mortgage payments from tenants and grow your portfolio. This allows you to create a mini real estate empire which you can use to lead a care-free lifestyle. However, getting there is the hard part. This book will teach you how to get your first rental properties.

Revelation #2: You Can Start With $0.

It's possible to start acquiring properties with $0 payment down or merely a few thousand dollars. Think you need to be a millionaire to become a landlord? Wrong! Rental income is far more risk-free than flipping income, as you could purchase the worst house and rent it out immediately – there's no need to repair the property. You don't have to spend money refurbishing the interior and you can get funding from private investors to purchase your rental property.

There are ways to convince financiers to finance your rental ventures in exchange for a monthly payment. Of course, the more money you have initially, the more money you'll get to keep in rental income at the end of each month. If you have a million dollars to spare, you could purchase multiple properties and start renting them out for serious income. If you have no money, you can reach out to private investors for funding or fund your properties via banking institutions. We'll show you the most viable methods to fund your rental properties for every budget.

Revelation #3: You Can Get Paid Every Week.

Tenants will deposit payments in your bank account every week or every month. Technically, you could purchase a property and rent it on a daily basis to tourists on AirBnb, if you're willing to deal with clients every day. Rental property has no restrictions on the type of tenants you're allowed to have. The safest rental scheme is to provide housing for the average American family that has 2.5 children and a dog. However, that doesn't restrict your income.

If you have a property in a central location with many amenities, you could charge three times the market average to rent to tourists. Depending on how much time you're willing to spend dealing with tenants, you can adjust your payment terms accordingly. If you are willing to deal with tenants every day, you could get paid by the day. If you want a stable check deposited in your account at the end of each month, you can rent out to families. The latter is safer, but less profitable. The only work you'll have to do is bi-monthly checkups and annual maintenance (property taxes, insurance payments, etc.).

Revelation #4: There Is Work Involved.

We won't lie to you - rental income requires a certain amount of work. You won't have to call in general contractors and stress on the property every day like a flipper, but you will have to do to the occasional repair. What if you get a call at 3 a.m. from a tenant who has a roof leak? You can't tell them "go fix it yourself". You have to hire a roofing contractor who can get the job done and deal with that contractor for possibly weeks at a time. You're legally obliged to repair the property or you could face legal prosecution with fines and possible jail time. If a tenant dies as a result of property maintenance, the burden is on you.

Each time a problem arises in one of your properties, you will get a call from the tenants and they'll expect you to show up and fix it. It's your duty to hire the contractors and ensure that living conditions in your properties are up to par with the standards imposed by your state. Like with any other business proposition, it's possible to skip the menial work. If you wish to disappear off the map, you could hire a "manager" do all the maintenance work for you and sail off into the sunset. However, most landlords live right next to their properties and assist tenants as problems arise due to trust issues. The most dedicated landlords in cities like New York own thousands of apartments and they attend to tenant's needs personally.

Revelation #5: Things Can Get Personal.

Have you ever rented your own apartment when you were a young adult and struggled to make payments? People run into financial distress all the time and your tenants won't be an exception. Certain landlords refuse to get close to their tenants and keep a business relationship in case they have to evict. Things can get ugly when you're dealing with tenants. Don't forget you're dealing with humans with real lives. The father renting from you might not be able to make rent after he's been fired from his job and the decision to evict him and his family will weigh on your conscience.

You'll have to make hard decisions. What if you're dealing with a single mother who has two babies to raise and she just lost her job and can't make rent? She may not realize that you still have to make your mortgage payments. Will you fall behind them or will you forgive their mortgage payment? You'll have to decide if you'll let them stay or if you'll evict them and make a place for new tenants. Landlord life is not glorious in many situations, despite how it's portrayed on TV shows. The more lower income your housing units are, the more you'll run into people with financial difficulties.

We'll give you the landlord secrets straight from the devil's mouth: We'll teach you how to finance properties, how to find tenants, and how to make a passive income with minimal work. Let's go!

Chapter 1 - Understanding Rental Property Investment

Why Rental Property?

Joe has $150,000 to invest. Why should Joe focus on rental properties instead of flipping properties? Rental is a whole different ball game. Rental properties are for the long term. For one, Joe can purchase a property he rents out without modifying the interior of the house. He can also start making a guaranteed profit as opposed to flipping a house that has to stay on the market for six months on average. Rental properties are for people who want long-term money, and who want to reap huge profits from depreciation. How many boomers do you know who bought a house for $100,000 in the 80's which is now worth over $1,000,000? If you hold on to your property for a decade or two, the value is guaranteed to double. In the meantime, you can get guaranteed monthly payments from tenants. We will teach you how to purchase properties, attract tenants, and get them to pay off your mortgages. For now, we'll show you why you need to invest in rental:

1) Real estate appreciation.

House prices in America go up. If you buy in a mid-sized city with population growth such as Austin, Texas, you're bound to see huge returns in as little as a few years. Appreciation means the property will increase in value the longer you hold on to it. People were able to purchase houses for a lot less than they cost today. The average $250,000 suburban house with a picket fence went for $100,000 in the 90s. What's not to say that the average $250,000 house of today will not be going for $500,000 within 15 years? The growth is bound to happen - you'll either buy in now or you'll miss out in the long run.

Even if you ignore guaranteed monthly payments for each property, purchasing a property in a hot area means you'll make hundreds of thousands (if not even millions) over the long term. Remember, it's yours when you buy it (not the tenant's). You can sell and get rid of a property at any time.

The city and market have an effect on the appreciation. Historically, the wealthiest cities in the U.S., such as New York City and San Francisco, experience appreciation cycles and the average apartment in these cities can go for over $1M. However, you don't need to buy in Midtown Manhattan to get appreciation. You could buy in suburban Portland, Oregon and still see significant returns in 15 years. The best cities in which to invest are mid-sized cities with strong population growth. Do you know which cities have the highest growth per capita? They're not NYC or LA. They're mid-sized cities with booming economies such as Seattle, Atlanta, Austin, and Charlotte.

To be upfront, you will not make a significant amount of money within the first few years. You might not make any money at all within the first 5 years. However, you will double your investment within the first 10 years even if you invest in the most average neighborhood in the United States. Any decent area with good access to schools and convenience stores will do. You don't need exceptional and the property doesn't have to stand out. Go for a drive, and you'll notice almost all houses are average houses. Those houses increase in value as the U.S. economy produces more wealth. Get in on the action now or miss out.

2) Cash Payments from Tenants.

The tenant has to pay you by the month – you'll get a guaranteed $1000-2000 a month in profits for the average property. If you haven't figured it out, the average mortgage tends to be lower than $1000 while rents for a house are typically higher. This is where you'll make returns in the short term. If you don't have any money at all, you can make enough to cover a down payment on a mortgage and finance a $150,000 house. Once you become the owner, if your mortgage payment is $900 a month, you can rent the house for $1500 a month. This means your mortgage will be paid off and you'll have a few hundred left to spare. The tenant has to pay all bills unless and they're essentially paying off your mortgage. What's better than getting guaranteed payments without doing any work? You only have to pay the down payment, which is typically 20%. If that doesn't convince you to get into rental properties, nothing will.

If you have investment money to spare, you will keep all the profits without making mortgage payments. The $1500/month rent money will go directly in your pocket and you won't have to pay off the bankers – your only expenses will be the house insurance and yearly property tax, which is rarely above 2% of the total value of the property. Moreover, you have other rental avenues that are open to you. You could rent the property on a daily basis and charge a higher markup for holidays such as Christmas, New Year's, etc. This allows you to make two to three times the average profits of a rental property in your area. All properties rent out immediately, without any repairs necessary. House-flippers have to invest tens of thousands of dollars bringing a property up to current standards, while landlords only have to throw the property on the market.

3) Tax Rebates.

The IRS thinks rental properties are not the most profitable form of property and they have write-offs for virtually every type of property. Landlords can claim "losses" every year and get deductions for all their income taxes, which helps them keep more of their rental income. Rental investments are IRS-safe because the property appreciates and depreciates simultaneously. The IRS believes that properties depreciate due to tear and wear, however, the market is usually on the upswing and the property value for properties tends to increase.

The IRS gives landlords write-offs under a specific property depreciation system called "General Depreciation System" or GDS. The GDS states that an average property has a recovery period of 27.5 years, which the IRS deems to be the average useful life of a property. The IRS provides deductions of precisely 3.6% per year on each building you own. In effect, the property taxes will be lower than the write-offs you're allowed. Using a simple write-off, you can pay the property tax and keep more of your profits using the GDS write-off.

4) Inflation Works In Your Favor.

Inflation raises the value of the property, while your mortgage payments remain the same. If you obtain a fixed-rate loan, which is the most popular of loans, you won't spend a single cent more than what you agreed to initially. For example, if you pay $20K as a down payment on a $100K property and that property appreciates to $200K within 10 years, you'll still only owe $80K. In effect, you only paid $20K to acquire a $200K property over 10 years. Inflation is your friend over the long-term and the fixed-priced mortgage allows you to only pay what you originally agreed to, instead of the inflated price of the property after you acquired it.

Two Ways to Earn Profits with Rental Property

1) Long Term Rentals

The safest and most conventional way to rent is long-term: You rent to families or professional individuals who have a job and the ability to make monthly payments. This is a foolproof rental method that requires monthly engagement with the tenant, only when you're collecting rent. You don't have to show up every week and check up on them and you only have to meet them when it's time to collect the rent. Long-term rent is the way to go, because families sign 6-month or 12-month contracts which are extendable.

You can progressively increase the rent as properties in your area increase in value and the neighborhood becomes more desirable. For example, a house that rented out for $1000 this year might go for $1250 next year. Tenants don't like the rent increase? You'll find new ones in one week. The beauty of rental properties is that multiple people are competing for the property and you always have a viable pool of tenants to choose from, even in the most low-income areas. Here's how to calculate your bottom-line profits:

The 1% Rule of Long-Term Rentals

The 1% rule is the simplest calculation people use to estimate the profitability of a rental property. You can estimate the profitability of a rental property before you even purchase the actual property, which will give you an indicator as to how much bottom-line profits you'll have left with at the end of each month. The 1% rule states the following: If the GROSS monthly rent makes up 1% of the original purchase price, you should buy the property. If the monthly rent before expenses is less than 1% of the original purchase price, you should seek out other properties.

Let's say you find a house in decent shape for $100,000. How do you know if you'll make a profit renting it out? Simple: Use the 1% rule. The 1% rule states that your gross rent should exceed 1% of the original purchase price. The property has to rent out for at least $1000 a month if you want to make a Return on Investment (ROI). Under this rule-of-thumb, a $100,000 property has to rent out for $1000 a month and bring in 12% of the original purchase price in returns annually. In this particular example, the $100,000 property has to return $12,000 in annual gross profits before expenses such as property insurance, taxes, and bills. Your net revenue needs to be 6-8% of the total property value per year. This means that when you rent long-term, you should be making returns of $6000-8000 per year in pure profits on a $100,000 property.

The average net return of 6-8% per year is a great deal, but it's going to depend on the city and neighborhood. The nicer the neighborhood, the lower the rental returns. The flipside is that a 6% return on a $300,000 house is higher than a 15% return on a $100,000 house. The highest rental returns typically found in cheap run-down properties exist because the properties cost little to purchase and the rental price is still relatively high. In general, you should be getting a solid 6% return in nice neighborhoods with affluent tenants and 8-10% returns on low-income neighborhoods with riskier properties that are more crime-prone. Whichever one you decide, you should not settle for less than 6% in yearly net returns.

The Capitalization Rate

Landlords calculate the "cap" rate, which is short for the capitalization rate, of the initial investment. The cap rate formula is the following:

Yearly Net Profits / Home Value = Cap Rate

Example: $8000 / $100,000 = 0.08

In this case, 0.08 is the result we're getting or 8% net ROI in simple terms. The capitalization rate on a $100,000 property which makes a net turnover of $8000 per year totals out to 8%. Whether 8% is a satisfactory return for the amount of effort you put into maintaining the property is up to you to decide.

The same principle applies to properties with a much higher property value. For example, if you find nice properties which give you an 8% cap rate on a $500,000 investment, you could make significant cash flow which pays off the property and gives you a great living. On the flip side, an 8% cap rate might not be worth it in a high-crime area that takes a lot to maintain and has extremely high insurance payments. In theory, you wouldn't need to be wealthy to finance a down payment on a $500,000 house, but you would have to save up for a few years.

2) Short-Term Rentals

Short-term rentals are the opposite of long-term rentals: They're unstable and they require constant work. You'll have to deal with clients a lot more than you would with long-term rentals, possibly daily. When you deal with long-term tenants, you only have to sign a contract and check them once or twice a month when it's time for you to collect your check or carry out the odd repair. With short term tenants, you have to meet tenants every day and clean up after them to prepare the property for the next tenants. What's in it for you? The markup is significantly higher. If you rent a house to a family for $1000 a month that wouldn't require any work on your end, but you'd only be left with $1000 at the end of each month. However, if you rent the same house for $100 a day to clients on AirBnb, you could make $3000 each month, but then you'd have to work and maintain the property every day.

Short-term rentals are the way to go if you have the time and patience to deal with clients on a daily basis. This is an excellent opportunity for young property owners or established property owners who enjoy meeting people and socializing. What's better than offering value to society and making huge returns in the process? You're not restricted to short-term rent from websites such as Craigslist and AirBnb. Once you own the property, you can convert it to a mini hotel or a hostel. It's possible to place four bunk beds in each room and convert the property to a hostel, then charge each one of the tenants $20 a night to stay there. This can generate a lot more cash flow than renting the property to a four-person family. Short-term rental requires a lot more work than long-term rental, but the profit margins are significantly higher.

Developing the Right Mindset for Rental Property Success

The one thing all landlords agree with is that they're in it for the profit. However, individual motives for obtaining profit may be different. Some people become landlords to retire and live out the rest of their lives in peace. Some people become landlords to escape their 9-5 job and be able to survive without slaving at a dead-end job. Entrepreneurs who are motivated to become wealthy typically purchase multiple properties and rent them out while waiting for a high-ticket payout. Others become landlords by accident, by inheriting a few properties and converting them to rental units. We all have to deal with tenants, enforce payments and perform scheduled maintenance work. The property won't maintain itself and someone has to make the insurance and tax payments.

The landlord life is not a straight path, and we're driven into it for many reasons. If you want to retire, you will have to invest more in the property because the property has to be rentable over an extended period such as over multiple decades. For this purpose, you should purchase the newest and most expensive property possible. If you want to become wealthy and you don't plan to hold out to properties for too long, you can purchase semi run-down properties and make a higher markup renting them out. The following mindset tricks will be detrimental to your success in the rental property business:

1) The Cash Flow Mindset

The most essential landlord mindset is to develop an emergency cash-flow mindset. The faster you gather the cash to purchase the property or put down a deposit, the faster you'll be able to get out of your dead-end 9-5 job and/or retire. Remember you never have to cover the full purchase price of the property and you can get away with paying as little as 20%. If the rental home costs $100,000 you will only have to finance $20,000. How hard is it to save up this amount in today's economy? Even if you live in your mom's basement and work a minimum wage job, you should be able to save up $20,000 and put down a deposit on your first rental property. Don't be afraid to do the dirty jobs and the low-paid jobs because you'll only have to work them until you can finance your first property. Get two jobs! The faster you get the money, the faster you'll be able to finance your properties and create a new life for yourself.

Your focus should be on acquiring as many properties as possible and increasing the cash flow. If you're young and determined, you can afford to do short-term rentals and place an emphasis on increasing cash flow to milk the properties for the maximum amount of dollars viable. If you're reaching retirement age, you need to gather the investment funds you'll need to put down a deposit for stable properties that will pay for your retirement. The landlord mindset is not only about choosing properties and dealing with tenants, it's also about having a sense of urgency and gathering money for new properties. The faster you get at obtaining capital, the more money returns you'll see coming your way.

2) The Enforcer Mindset

The ugly truth about rental properties is that you'll have to deal with real human beings who might not be able to make rent - therefore you'll have to apply discipline and boundaries to make sure you're paid on time. This is especially critical during the first few months when you're getting established and missing a single payment could mean your property is one call away from being repossessed. You'll have to learn how to make your clients pay on time. In effect, you're becoming an enforcer that has to enforce the lease agreement.

What do you do when a tenant misses a payment? The tenant won't care that you have to make mortgage payments on the home; they'll only care for their individual situation. This is why the minute they fail to make a payment, you must file a late rent reminder. This reminder should go out in the first day they don't make a timely payment. The reminder has to have "grace period", which is the time they're allowed to go before they get an eviction warning.

If the tenant fails to pay in the grace period, you should file an eviction notice. The eviction notice notifies the tenant that civil court eviction action will be taken against them. The tenants will come to you with personal stories, but you shouldn't bend and give them leeway because they'll continue asking for more time. If you allow leeway once, they will know that your time is not important. If the landlord doesn't care, why should the tenants pay on time? Only give leeway when you don't have to make mortgage payments or it would compromise your personal relationship with a family member.

1)   The Discipline Mindset

As a landlord you're not only supposed to perform monthly maintenance tasks where you greet your tenants, check up on the property, and collect rent. You must also carry out semi-annual and annual administrative tasks that require discipline and advance planning. What if you get hit with a $4000 bill on a roof leak? You'll need to prepare in advance. This takes discipline. Instead of spending your net profits on cruises in the Caribbean, set them aside for unexpected bills.

The lease terms should be drafted by a lawyer and have a paragraph mentioning a clause for semi-annual inspections which grant you the right to access the property. The properly won't need to have structural damage to warrant an inspection. The landlord shouldn't wait for things to go wrong before inspecting a property. Identify problems in advance and fix them! Make sure that your values are communicated clearly. If you don't tolerate smoking inside the property, you have to be prepared to evict a tenant if you detect smoke. Better yet, get a non-smoker tenant while you're signing the agreement.

Regular maintenance ensures that the property is well-mainlined and that your tenants don't experience problems inhabiting the property. The inspection is not only for property damage but unauthorized pets and people living on the property. While you're carrying out inspections, build up a personal relationship with your tenants. Feel free to ask them about their children, jobs, lives, etc.

Don't forget to raise the rent every year when the lease terms expire. Many landlords worry about raising rents. If you refuse to raise rents, your income will fall behind the market value and won't keep up with inflation. Raise the rents when the lease expires instead of raising it surprisingly at random times during the year, which scares tenants. This way you'll give them the option to pay higher rent prices or find a new property.

Chapter 2—Great Location, Great Investment

Now that we've given you a brief understanding of rental property investments, it's time to tell you about the different classes of real estate, what kinds of properties you can invest in, how you can evaluate target neighborhoods, and how you can identify emerging real estate markets that can generate large profits.

Classes of Real Estate, Where You Should Invest.

If you're going to get involved in the real estate market, you're going to need to familiarize yourself with the way different properties are classified or grouped. Although these classifications are somewhat subjective and there are no universal classifications or guidelines for how to identify properties, we can offer you some guidelines which should be helpful to you in grading specific locations or buildings. Real estate is often classified or graded similar to the way many of us were graded in high school or college, a letter grading system. These grading systems can go from A to C, A to D, A to F. A is obviously the highest rating; F is the poorest rating.

With real estate, the location often receives one rating and the building receives another rating. For example, if you have a great building in a mediocre area, you would have an A building in a C area. If you have an uninhabitable building in a questionable area, you would have an F building in a D area. Following are descriptions on how most people categorize locations with this grading system.

An A location is in an area with the newest buildings, the hottest restaurants, and the best schools. You get the picture. It is an area that will have the highest rents.

An A building is a building that is most likely less than 10 years old. These buildings are likely to have the latest in granite countertops, hardwood floors, etc.

Rental properties in these A areas are likely to be high rent, low maintenance properties. They're easy investments, however it should also be noted that they may also bring a lower return on investment because of the higher demand and higher purchase price.

The B location is often in an area that has decent restaurants, albeit not the trendiest or most expensive restaurants. The schools are good, but not the brand new schools that some of the posh areas have. The area is home to mostly middle class, certainly more blue collar than the A areas. The people living in the B areas are much more likely to be living check to check.

The buildings in the B location are older, usually 15 to 30 years old. Most of these buildings have been upgraded, however not with the amenities of the A buildings.

As an investor in B properties, you'll find that they're likely to require more maintenance and attention than an A property would require. These properties will rent for less than A properties, but they are also capable of bringing you larger profits, because of the more moderate purchase price.

The C locations are marginal locations, often locations that are 30 years or older. The C buildings are often outdated and antiquated, in need of many and frequent repairs. C buildings often require plumbing and electrical upgrades; these buildings often require lots of attention and tender loving care. The upside of these C buildings is that they can often be purchased at a very moderate price; the downside is the amount of money you will likely have to spend to maintain or upgrade them.

D locations are dilapidated areas, often crime-infested and possibly dangerous. These are areas with many vacant or boarded up buildings. The buildings there are either neglected or uninhabitable. Unless you are a seasoned real estate investor, you'll probably want to stay away from investing in these areas. You would really have to know what you're doing to make money from a D building in a D area.

An F building and/or an F location can best be identified as a war zone. Crime-infested, drug-infested, struggling schools, homes and apartments in complete disrepair, etc. You get the picture; nothing that you should be interested in as a novice real estate investor.

Four Important Factors for Evaluating a Neighborhood.

Now that we've outlined the different classes of real estate, it's time to take a look at the different factors involved in evaluating the locations or areas in which you should invest. You've probably heard it before...there three major factors in real estate success: location, location, and location. Yes, that's an old cliché, but it still rings true. Location is almost always going to be the most important factor in the profitability of your real estate investments.

Most rental property investor newbies invest in properties which are near where they live. They do this because they are already familiar with the area, and also because properties in the near vicinity offer easy access for many of the responsibilities involved in rental property: showing the property, maintaining the property, rent collection, etc. Although owning rental property in the same area you live is most advantageous, there is a possible downside. If the economy in your area declines or tanks, you'll have all your eggs in one basket. If all your properties are in one area, they'll all be subject to the same factors which could affect the devaluation of the property, including a declining economy, increasing crime rates, weather disaster events (flooding, tornadoes and hurricanes, earthquakes), etc.

Here are some of the major factors for evaluating an area for possible rental property investment:

1)   Employment rate. What's the employment rate in the area in which you are thinking of investing? That will have a major impact on how successful you can be with a rental property in that area. Obviously, if the unemployment rate in that area is high, you may find that it's an area in which it's going to be difficult to find and maintain reputable renters.

2)   Crime rate. The crime rate in the area is also going to be a factor in whether you're going to be able to secure and keep renters. Major crimes such as homicides, sexual assaults, burglaries, robberies, and auto theft are certain to tarnish the reputation and livability of an area and those crimes and the reputation that follows them may impact your chance for success in that area or location.

3)   School system. Does the area you're considering have a good school system? If you are going to be renting to families with kids, the school system in the area may impact your ability to rent a property. If the area has a good school system, you're likely to find that people will want to live in that area because of that. On the other hand, if the reputation of the area school system is lacking, you may find that people are looking to move out of the district.

4)   Vacancy/No Vacancy. Is the area you're considering for rental property an area that has a lot of vacancies? Or are there barely any vacancies? This will also be an indicator of the possible success you might have in the area. If there are a lot of vacancies in your area, commercial and residential, you're going to find it much more difficult to rent a property in that area. And you're likely to find that rental rates have much lower profit margins, as the market is much more competitive. If you drive through the neighborhood and find that many businesses or homes are boarded up or vacant, that's not a good sign. On the other hand, if you drive through the area and find that many residences or businesses are remodeling, that's a sign that people are investing in the area.

How to Spot an Emerging Real Estate Market.

If you're going to invest in rental properties, you're going to want to look for emerging real estate markets instead of submerging real estate markets. There are a number of sure indicators as to whether a market is flourishing or struggling. Although a lot of this information can be found online, you should not underestimate the value of finding out information on these areas by simply visiting the area and by meeting with the people who live and work in the area. Although data and analytics are important in making real estate decisions, you should never disregard the "eye test" as part of your decision making.

One determinant to consider in your real estate investments is the population growth of the area. Is the area growing, is it stable or stagnant, is it declining? Obviously, population growth and the corresponding demand for housing is desirable for real estate investors. You'll likely want to tie yourself to an area that is growing in selecting the areas in which you own real estate.

Another factor to consider is existing home sales. Even if an area appears to be economically depressed, an increase in existing home sales can be a strong indicator that an area is reemerging or coming back. As a real estate investor, you need to be aware that areas and neighborhoods often regenerate themselves and if you can get into these areas early in the process, you'll stand to make a lot more profit than you would if you are a latecomer. That being said, some areas and neighborhoods never regenerate and it will be important for you to identify these areas as you decide whether or not to invest in them. Existing home sales within the area are a key indicator to the possible vitality of the area. When reviewing statistics for any area, it is important to note that you'll need to fine tune these statistics as much as possible. For example, if you are looking at making a real estate investment in the Atlanta area, it's important for you to refine that information to a smaller area. Atlanta is a large metropolitan area and there are neighborhoods within that area that are flourishing and other neighborhoods that are struggling at any given time. So, you will need to certainly refine your information search down to a zip code or preferably even a neighborhood within a zip code.

Rising rental rates are another strong indicator in spotting an emerging real estate market. If rental rates are increasing steadily year after year, this is an indication that the real estate market within the area is healthy and a possible target for investment. If you're interested in determining rental rates in a given area, Zillow's rent index provides valuable information, including the median estimated market rate rent across any specific region and housing type.

Also, new construction within an area is an indicator that the area is healthy from a real estate standpoint. The Residential Construction Index provided by the U.S. Census Bureau contains valuable information about the number of building permits which are issued for a particular area and also the number of new homes which are started and completed each month.

Foreclosure rates within any given area are another indicator of real estate investment potential. As someone interested in rental property, you'll probably want to steer clear of areas that have increasing foreclosure rates.

Also, there are less conventional factors which might indicate whether an area is a good target for investment. Has a large company announced that it is relocating to the area or that it is opening a branch in the area? If so, it follows that the employees at this new location will be relocating also. Some of them will be looking to move closer to their workplace. Either way, that can only be good for the economy of the area. On the downside, has a large employer announced that they will be leaving the area? If so, this move is likely to have a negative impact on the local economy.

Another less conventional indicator of real estate rental potential is to determine the normal amount of time it takes for a house to be sold or rented. If that average time frame is over six months, that may well be an indicator that the market is flat and not a good candidate for current investment. On the other hand, if those homes are selling or renting in 30 days, that is a very good sign and it's an indicator that the area is a good investment target.

Chapter 3—Choosing the Best Property

Now that you know more about how to evaluate properties and areas and how to identify areas that are good investment targets, it's time to talk about how to choose the types of real estate investments which will work best for you. This is an important part of the process, as some retail estate investor wannabes make the mistake of choosing an area of real rental that does not fit their interests or their personality.

Residential Real Estate to Invest In

You may be surprised to learn that there are many different types of real estate to invest in, including a number of different types of residential real estate:

1) **Single family homes.** These are the most popular type of rental homes. Although single family homes also include some of the other types of homes listed below (apartment, condos, townhomes, coops, luxury homes, vacation homes), single family homes are the largest category of residential real estate.

2) **Condominiums/coops.** Although condos and coops are single family homes, they are a bit different in that they are managed by a homeowner's association. The homeowner's association is often responsible for the common areas and responsibilities for the complex, including garbage collection, landscaping, common area maintenance, and often exterior maintenance of the individual units. In return, the homeowner's association collects a fee from all members. If you are going to rent out a unit that is managed by a homeowner's association, you'll have to incorporate the homeowner's fees into the rent amount you charge your tenants.

3) **Multi-family homes.** Multi-family units are properties that include two or more dwellings which are rented out separately. This includes apartment building, duplexes, and triplexes. With some real estate investors, the owner is living in one of the units and is then renting out the other units. Owning multi-family homes is slightly more complicated than owning single family homes, as the performance of the property is based on the performance of each unit individually. Also, you should know that multi-family homes are sometimes classified as commercial properties, depending on the number of units involved.

4) **Luxury homes.** Luxury homes are top-quality homes which contain the latest amenities, technologies, and appliances. These are properties that demand top-dollar rental rates. And they are the most expensive homes to invest in.

5) **Vacation homes.** Vacation homes are often rented out on a seasonal basis, with the rental rates fluctuating from high during the peak season to lower during non-peak season. Most vacation homes are located in tourist areas. Areas in Texas, Florida, and Arizona have plenty of vacation homes to accommodate "snowbirds", people from northern areas of the U.S. trying to escape the cold weather and snow of the winters. Investors also own vacation homes along the coasts in various locations. Others own vacation homes near tourist destinations such as Disney World. And lake homes in the northern areas of the country such as Minnesota, Michigan, and Wisconsin, can also be good investments. One of the advantages of owning a vacation property is that the owners will often use these properties for their own vacations or getaways and then rent out the property for the remainder of the year.

Types of Commercial Real Estate

Commercial real estate covers a lot of different types of real estate, all the way from single office buildings or spaces to massive skyscrapers, airports, stadiums, amusement parks, and shopping malls. As a real estate rental newbie, we're going to presume that you're closer to the lower end of investors, but you should know that almost all of the types of commercial real estate we're listing include both small and large properties. Because of the costs involved, commercial real estate is almost always a higher stakes game. By the same token, most commercial leases are longer than residential leases, because of the accommodations which are normally made to the building or the property for the tenants.

1)   Office space. This is the most common commercial property. The office space spectrum ranges from single tenant properties to skyscrapers and office complexes which are home to hundreds of tenants and thousands of their employees. Like residential properties, commercial properties are classified on grade levels (i.e.—A, B, C). Class A commercial real estate consists of new buildings or recently refurbished/extensively refurbished buildings. They are normally in excellent areas and normally managed by professional management companies. Class B commercial real estate is the most popular class for investors. Class B properties are generally slightly older buildings that require some capital investment for minor repairs or upgrades. Class C commercial properties are often old buildings that are targeted for major renovations or redevelopment. Those who invest in Class C properties can generally expect major capital investments to bring the property up-to-date and to make it marketable to tenants. Vacancy rates are usually much higher for Class C properties and these properties are much more difficult to lease.

2)   Retail. Again, the spectrum range is huge, ranging from a print shop that might have two or three employees to a restaurant or bank that might have 50 employees to a huge shopping mall that might have thousands of employees. Retail properties are often located in urban areas or business districts. Most shopping malls are owned by large investment groups, but on the lower end of the spectrum, some of the smaller retail locations are owned by single, mom-and-pop, or family investors.

3)   Industrial. Industrial properties range from manufacturing facilities to warehouse facilities. They often require larger amounts of space to accommodate dock areas for shipments that come in and go out. These industrial properties are generally in lower rent, lower traffic areas, as they are lower profile businesses that do not require prime real estate.

4)   Multi-family. This includes residential locations that have as few as four units. It also includes large apartment complexes and high-rise condominium complexes. Many residential property investors who want to get into commercial real estate choose to get into commercial real estate by investing in multi-family properties such as apartment buildings that can accommodate anywhere from four to a dozen tenants. As we discuss commercial real estate in this chapter, it should be pointed out that residential leases are often much shorter than commercial leases. Most residential leases have six or 12-month terms. Most commercial leases will range from three to 20 years, depending on the building and the business. Commercial leases are normally longer because the owner often has to make accommodations to the building in order to fit the tenant's business. And then when that tenant leaves, the building or space generally has to be repurposed or remodeled to fit the next tenant.

5)   Special purpose. As long as we just mentioned repurposing, we should also mention special purpose commercial real estate. This is generally a building that is built for a unique or special purpose and can not often be repurposed without a lot of renovation. Businesses such as car washes, schools, and storage facilities are considered special purpose locations. For example, if you own a property and are leasing to a tenant who has a car wash, it's not going to be easy to repurpose that building if and when the tenant leaves. You're either going to have to lease to another tenant who wants to use the facility as a car wash or you're going to have to be prepared to make major accommodations or renovations for the next tenant. That's why leases for special purpose buildings are generally much longer than leases for other types of commercial real estate.

And while we're discussing special purpose commercial real estate, we should also mention mixed use developments. These developments have become extremely popular in recent years, mostly in urban areas. An example of a mixed use development would be a multiple story apartment complex with a business or businesses on the ground floor. That business might be a pizza restaurant, a health club, or even a supermarket. Generally, the business located on the ground floor of the complex is a retail location which can benefit financially from the tenants above. Along the same lines, large corporations have mixed use buildings in which their offices constitute a large amount of the space, but then they lease the remaining space to other retail businesses who can benefit from the large number of employees. As an example, a large corporation in the electronics industry has a campus with multiple buildings and thousands of employees. They allow certain retail companies to rent space within their building, including coffee companies, a dry cleaners, a health club, and a doctor's office. The feeling is that not only can these businesses benefit from the corporation's large numbers of employees, the corporation is also making things more convenient for employees who no longer need to leave the premises for some of their errands or activities.

6) **Owner occupied.** Some real estate investors purchase property with the intent of using it for their own purposes. And some of these investors will use a portion of the space for themselves and then rent out other portions to tenants. This strategy can be applied to many of the commercial real estate options discussed above.

The 1% Rule for Investing in Real Estate

We previously mentioned the 1% Rule. As you consider which real estate investments to make, you'll need to use some kind of measurement tool to determine how much rent you would need to charge for a property, commercial or residential. You'll need to make sure that the rent you are charging your tenants will at least cover all of your expenses for the property; hopefully more, so you can make a profit. After all, most of us do not intend to get into the real estate business as a hobby; most of us are looking to make a profit. The 1% rule for investing is one way you can determine how much rent you'll need to charge for any rental property you invest in. Here's how it works. (Excuse us for being a bit redundant, but it's absolutely imperative that you have a measurement tool for the amount of rent you'll need to charge to derive income from the property.)

With the 1% rule, you simply multiply the purchase price of the property by 1% to determine the base level of the monthly rent you will need to charge. For example, if you purchase a property for $300,000, you'll multiply that by 1% to get a base rate of $3000. That $3000 will be the base you should work from in determining a rent level from a tenant. But please know that this is just the base level and you will also need to consider other expenses for the property, including things such as insurance, taxes, and upkeep. Upkeep can include things such as garbage collection, janitorial services, snow removal, and landscaping. Those expenses will also need to be accounted for as you work to determine your rent level and your break-even point.

Obviously, the rent or rents you are charging need to cover your mortgage payments (unless you are indeed investing in real estate as a charity or a hobby.) If the property you are interested in will require any major repairs or renovations before it can be leased, you'll need to add those cost estimates to the purchase price before you calculate the 1%. For example, if the $300,000 property you're interested in will require a $20,000 roof repair before it is marketable, you'll add that $20,000 before you divide by 1%. As an investor, you should ideally seek a mortgage loan with monthly payments that are less than the 1% figure you've calculated.

Again, there are many other factors to consider in evaluating the profit potential of a property, but the 1% rule at least gives you a base to work from in determining what rent level you would need to charge and what kind of mortgage payments you should look for in purchasing the property.

Essential Questions to Keep in Mind When Evaluating Property

Investing in real estate for rental is a major consideration and you'll need to make sure you ask yourself the correct questions in evaluating any property. Here are some questions you should be asking as you consider purchasing rental properties:

1)   Will the location make for a solid investment? As mentioned before, location might be the major factor in whether a rental property is profitable. In evaluating any location, there are a number of things to consider. Is the location near to amenities that your prospective tenants are going to require? If you're planning to rent to young families with kids, nearby amenities such as good schools, supermarkets, gyms, and restaurants will enhance your investment. If you are planning to rent to senior citizens, nearby amenities such as supermarkets, doctors' offices and medical clinics, and health clubs will be attractive to prospective renters. If you are thinking of renting to college students, nearby bars, restaurants, and gyms may enhance the attractiveness of your property. Another thing to consider with location is whether the area contains a large enough pool of prospective renters. For example, if you have an upscale property in an area where mostly middle class workers reside, you may have difficulty renting that property. If you have a low-rent Class C property in an area that is predominantly upscale residents, you may have difficulty renting. So, make sure that your location matches the pool of prospective renters you're targeting. If you can make sure your pool of prospective tenants matches your property, you'll ensure that you have consistent rental income over the time you own the property.

2)   Is the property functional? If not, what's it going to take to make it functional? It's okay to buy a property that needs repairs, even major repairs. However, before you purchase such a property, you'll have to determine how much it's going to cost and how long it's going to take to make the property functional. Novice investors are notorious for underestimating the costs involved in fixing up a property. We've heard some people say that if you are estimating costs and time frame for a property you should simply take whatever figures you come up with and double them. They live by the mantra, "If something can go wrong, it's likely to go wrong." So, if they have calculated renovation costs of $20,000, they'll be thinking that they could end up spending up to $40,000 for the renovation. If they calculate six weeks to do the renovation, they'll be aware that they renovation could take up to three months if things don't go as planned.

In evaluating the property you're interested in, you will have to determine what items you can fix yourself and what items you'll have to hire contractors for. And then you'll have to secure quotes for the work from those contractors. And obviously, you'll also have to price out materials costs for any renovation. This can be a somewhat complicated process; that's why many novice rental real estate investors will opt to purchase properties which do not require major renovations. They'll take the attitude that at least they have a better indication of what they are getting into as far as costs are concerned. If you're not experienced in renovating properties, you're more likely to stumble upon some expensive surprises in fixing up a property.

Also, you should know that when we are referring to a functional property, we are also referring to a property that is easily rentable to tenants and one that is safe for tenants. If these things aren't happening, you'll limit your ability to rent the property or you may endanger a tenant to the point where you are risking their safety or risking a serious insurance claim against you. For example, if you have a leaky roof, that will almost surely impact your ability to rent the property or, even, if you rent it, may jeopardize your ability to keep renting the property. Or, if your roof is in total disrepair, you might actually endanger the safety of a tenant.

3)   **What's it going to cost to maintain the property?**   In evaluating the viability or possible profitability of a rental property, you'll also need to determine what it is going to cost to maintain it. For example, if you own a small office complex, you're probably going to have to pay for landscaping and garbage collection. If you have common areas in the building, you'll have to pay for janitorial services, including restroom maintenance. If you're in a northern area, you'll probably have to pay for snow plowing or removal. All of these maintenance costs will have an impact on the profitability of your rental property. And you should note that there may be more costs involved in some rentals than in others. For example, if you are renting out a vacation property that turns over tenants frequently, you'll have to pay more to frequently prepare the property for new tenants. If you are renting a property to college students who may use it as a party

house, you may have to pay higher damage or repair costs as you prepare for new tenants. Is the property close to where you are living or working? Will you be willing to make any minor repairs yourself or will you need to hire a management company to handle these repairs? Those are all things to think about when you are evaluating the viability of a rental property.

Besides repair and routine maintenance costs, you'll have to ask yourself some other questions regarding the viability of the property. What are the expected property taxes? Projected insurance costs? What are the vacancy rates for the area the property is located in? How will you accommodate vacancy expenses? Will you have a separate fund set up for that or will you have to borrow money for that? (Hopefully, not the latter.) Is the rent amount you'll have to charge for the property competitive with rates being charged for similar properties in the same area? Is the property locating in a flourishing area? Declining area? Are there any changes coming to the area that will impact the economy? (i.e.—A major company coming to the area or leaving the area? Light rail or other major transportation routes coming to the area? A sports stadium coming to the area? This might impact parking availability in the area and make a residential property less desirable. On the other hand, it might also offer more opportunities in regards to commercial real estate for new restaurants, bars, and hotels.

Buying an investment property can be complicated. The upside is that rental property can also be very profitable. But you'll want to make sure that you've asked yourself all the necessary questions before you invest in any property. Miscalculating any of these factors could well make the difference between being profitable or losing money on your investment.

Chapter 4—Financing Your Rental Property

We've been talking about why owning rental property is a good idea, the different types of rental property investments to consider, and things to consider in choosing a rental property. Now it's time to tell you about the ways you can finance a rental property. There are multiple ways to do this, including some ways for first-time investors to enter the market.

House Hacking: Make Money and Live for Free

Some of you may not be familiar with the term "house hacking", so before we get into how to do it, we should explain what it is. House hacking involves the renting or leasing of owner-occupied properties to tenants in an effort to subsidize the occupany costs for the owner. House hacking is particularly popular with young, single investors. Here's how it works. A person will purchase a home (or office location) with the intention to live in that home. They'll then rent that home out to one or more occupants and use that rental income to subsidize or finance the cost of the property. As an example, a recent college grad opts to buy a starter home and then share it with two roommates. His mortgage payment is $1100 a month and he charges each of his roommates $600 a month in rent to cover the cost of his mortgage and some of the additional costs of the house, including water and electric. In essence, the recent college grad is able to live in the home for free, and at the same time, have his tenants pay for the equity he accumulates in the home.

The upside for the roommates is that they pay less to live in his home than they would to rent a one bedroom apartment. At the same time, they have more space and possibly more amenities than they would get with a one bedroom apartment.

The possible downside to the owner is that he has share his living quarters and he may prefer more privacy. (On the other hand, he may enjoy the company.) As most of us who have shared a living area know, the living arrangement will work much better if the parties are compatible. Also, there may be some security risks if you rent to a stranger. We've heard the story of a man who shared his home with a roommate, only to come home one day to find that all of his major belongings had disappeared.

It should also be pointed out that house hacking doesn't always involve roommates. It's not uncommon for some house hackers to purchase duplexes or triplexes, living in one of the units and then renting out the other units to others. This affords the owner a lot more privacy than he would receive in sharing a unit with roommates.

Let's outline the benefits of house hacking:

1)   You can decrease or eliminate your housing expense. As you all know, for most of us, our housing expensive is usually our largest monthly expense. Statistics show that Americans spend about 40% of their income on housing. In house hacking, you will be able to substantially reduce or eliminate those expenses. And for the recent college grads who are living with parents, house hacking also offers more independence than you'll have cohabiting with your parents.

2)   Increase your income, savings. Many people look at the house hacking stage as a transitional stage or temporary stage which allows them to work toward their own financial independence while they pay off school or car loans or save money toward the next home after the starter home. Some people will house hack as they work toward a second investment property; others will simply use the money to pay for a nice vacation.

3) **Get some experience as a landlord.** Living with tenants will allow you to get your feet wet in the world of being a landlord. In listening to the wants, needs, and concerns of your tenants, you'll get an inkling of what it's like to be a landlord. You'll also get an inkling of the things that can go wrong for a landlord (roof leaks, tenant late on the rent, refrigerator stops working, etc.). When repairs are required, you'll learn to solve problems, either by repairing the items yourself or enlisting someone to do the repairs for you.

4) **Owning property.** In owning property as a house hacker, you'll be establishing equity on the property. At the same time, your investment value may be escalating and when you go to sell the property, you'll reap the benefits of the escalated value.

Creative Ways to Finance Your Rental Properties

The conventional way to purchase a rental property is to save up for the down payment and then secure a mortgage to cover the remaining amount. There are however some other ways you can finance the purchase of a rental property.

1) **House Hacking.** As outlined above, house hacking is a popular way to finance your first rental property.

2) **Seller Financing.** Some sellers are willing to loan money for the purchase of their property. Some of them are willing to loan the entire amount of the purchase; others are willing to loan the down payment amount. If you can do this, you might find that it is a much simpler process than a bank loan with less paperwork. As someone who is buying the property, you'll want to make sure that you are getting a fair interest rate for the purchase. Unless you're very experienced in purchasing real estate properties, you will be well advised to consult with an attorney and/or CPA in initiating this purchase. And whatever you do, make sure you get your agreement in writing. For many of you, this will be one of the largest purchases of your life and you will certainly want to make sure that it is properly documented.

In discussing seller financing, you should know that many sellers do not advertise that they offer financing. If you are truly interested in seller financing as an option, you should ask the seller if they are willing to offer financing. It's possible that the seller hasn't thought about this before and you may find that they are so interested to sell the property that they will be willing to offer you financing at a good rate.

3)   Partnerships. If you don't have enough money for a down payment, you might secure a partner in your purchase. Do you have a friend or family member who would be willing to partner with you in purchasing a rental property? Although you can structure a partnership agreement any way you want, you should know that with a lot of real estate partnership agreements, one partner will make the down payment and then the other partner will handle all of the landlord duties, including collecting rent, making or arranging repairs, corresponding with tenants, etc. In essence, the person making the down payment is generally a silent partner. In return for the down payment, the two partners then agree to split the profits derived from the rental income and also when the property is sold. Again, these partnership agreements can be structured any way you and your partner want, but the basic tenet of the partnership is that one partner will provide the funds while the other will do the work.

Many partnerships are limited liability companies (LLCs) in which you can specifically outline your agreement and the corresponding roles and responsibilities of each party. LLCs are great in that they will also allow you to protect your personal assets in the event your business or partnership is ever sued. As we recommend previously in regards to seller financing, all partnership agreements should be outlined in writing. Verbal agreements and handshake agreements are not advised for such a major purchase. If you don't have a relationship with an attorney who can initiate an LLC or partnership agreement for you, companies such as Rocket Lawyer or LegalZoom are available online to help you draft simple legal agreements.

4)   Government programs. You may or may not be familiar with FHA, the Federal Housing Administration.   The FHA offers reasonable loans for owner-occupied properties, including single homes, duplexes, triplexes, and quadruplexes or four-unit apartment buildings. The loan rate for FHA loans is very reasonable at 3-1/2%. Loan limits for FHA loans are different in every county, so, if you're interested in FHA financing, we suggest that you find out what the loan limit is in your county before you get too far along in your search for rental investment properties.

5)   Retirement accounts. If you're a bit older and you have some retirement accounts you can draw from, this is another good way to finance the purchase of a rental property. If you have a self-directed IRA (Individual Retirement Account), you're not restricted to traditional assets such as stocks or mutual funds. You're also allowed to invest those funds in non-traditional assets, including rental property.   Again, we're going to suggest that you consult with a professional in using retirement accounts funds for a real estate purchase, whether that is a financial planner or a certified public accountant. Purchasing a rental property is serious business and you should not try to do so without professional counsel, unless you are experienced at doing so.

Start Saving for a Down Payment Right Now

As someone who is already this far into the book, it seems as if you have a sincere interest in purchasing and owning a rental property. That being said, you may be asking yourself how in the world you're ever going to accumulate the amount you'll need to actually purchase that property. In this chapter, we've outlined some simple thoughts on how you can save enough money to make a down payment. Most of these ideas are financial planning techniques that can be successful for anyone who is looking to save enough money for any particular purchase.

1)   The Percentage Plan. In using the percentage plan, we encourage you first to determine where all of your income is normally being spent. We suggest that you detail all of your mandatory or fixed expenditures within the past 90 days. Mandatory or fixed expenditures will be payments you have to make and will include things such as rent, utilities, school and car loans, food, gas, cable television, internet services, cell phone, etc. These payments should be easy to track, as you'll have receipts for most of them. Although some of these payments will vary slightly from month to month (i.e.—Your electric bill might be $60 one month and $70 another month), you should have enough information to figure out what your average monthly expenditure is. You'll then place all of these mandatory or fixed expenses in one category and move to the next category, which we'll call discretionary spending.

Discretionary spending covers remaining expenses that aren't necessary expenditures—things such as health club or gym memberships, the daily cup of joe you get from your neighborhood coffee shop, bar/restaurant/entertainment expenses, weekend getaways and vacations, etc. After you've listed all of the discretionary expenditures you can remember, you should then review these expenditures and see if any of them could be eliminated without severely cramping your lifestyle. Are you using your gym membership? Can you do without the daily cup of coffee from the neighborhood coffee shop? Do you really need to eat at restaurants three times a week? Can you do without a weekend getaway? Do you really need the premium cable tv package or could you make do with the less expensive basic package? In listing all of your discretionary expenses for the past 90 days, you'll be able to see how you are spending your money. If you can eliminate or reduce any of your discretionary expenditures, you should then be able to allocate these funds toward saving for a rental property down payment.

After you've totaled your fixed expenditures and determined what your discretionary expenditures should be, you should calculate what portion of your income each of these two categories accounts for. Most people find that fixed expenditures account for anywhere from 50 to 70 percent of their income. Your fixed expenditures are mostly non-negotiable. Maybe you can cut a small amount off your cable tv package by dropping some of the premium channels. Maybe you can carpool or consolidate your errands to save on gas expenditures. But for the most part, your fixed expenditures are what they are.

Your discretionary expenditures are exactly as described…they're discretionary. You should determine exactly which of these expenditures you can't do without and which of those you could either eliminate or reduce. After you've determined the amount you want to allocate on a monthly basis for discretionary activities, you should then see what percentage of your income these expenditures entail. And then see how much is left over for savings.

Some people will end up with a 70/20/10 plan. (70% fixed, 20% discretionary, 10% savings.) Others will end up with a 50/30/20 plan. You'll go with whatever works best for you, however the important thing is the savings category, as you'll use those funds to make the down payment on your rental property.

In setting a monthly limit for you discretionary spending, you will be able to save an accumulate the funds necessary to purchase your rental property. Are you an impulse spender? If so, you're the type of person who is likely to have the most difficulty in controlling your discretionary spending. If this is the case and you need help in controlling your monthly expenditures, there are apps that can help you do so. *Mint* is a popular app which can help you with your discretionary spending by alerting you when you are nearing the monthly limit you've assigned to your discretionary spending. When you get a "warning" that you're near your limit, maybe that warning will help you dial back your Amazon purchases or your Starbuck's coffee purchases.

Again, there's no set rule on how to set up your own income percentage plan. Whatever works for you should be fine, as long as you're setting aside a monthly amount you'll need for the down payment on your rental property.

2)   Reverse Engineer. Another way you can determine how long it's going to take you to save for your rental property down payment is to work backwards using reverse engineering. In doing so, you'll first determine the approximate price of the property you'll be looking to buy. For purposes of this example, we'll use $100,000 as the number to work with. We realize that this number may be extremely low for certain areas of the country, but it is an easy number to work with, especially for the mathematically impaired. Ha.

So, if, for example, you're thinking of purchasing a $100,000 property, you'll know that you'll have a 20% down payment on that property ($20,000). In addition to the down payment, you'll have closing costs that normally range from 1-2% of the down payment. You'll also need a contingency fund of maybe another 1-2%. For purposes of this example, let's keep it simple and list both the closing costs and the contingency/rainy day fund at $2000 each. So, coupled with the $20,000 down payment, you will need approximately $24,000 to purchase a $100,000 property. If you want to purchase the rental property in two years, you'll then divide the $24,000 total amount by

24 months. This will show you that you will need to save $1000 a month to reach your two-year savings goal. If this is too ambitious, you can always change your savings plan from 24 to 30 or 36 months. Or you can make the decision to look for less expensive/lower-priced properties. Again, there is no set prescription for how to establish a savings plan. You'll have to decide what works best for you or what you can live with. The goal of these savings plans is simply to get you to do the math in determining what it will take to accumulate the funds to purchase a rental property and then to put a plan into action.

3)   Automate Your Budget. It's no secret that lack of will power is the most common deterrent to any budget. You resolve to control your spending at the beginning of the month and then a few days into the month you find the signed National Football League jersey you've been looking for on ebay or the designer bag you've been looking for on Amazon. So much for the budget you set up at the start of the month. Five days in and you've already blown your discretionary budget limit. If this is you and if you have difficulty controlling impulse purchases, you might consider automating your payments, especially your savings payments.

If, after reviewing your expenditures, you've determined that you can save $750 a month, go ahead a set up an automatic payment once or twice a month from your checking account to a separate savings account you've designated for your rental property purchase. You should have a good idea as to when you get paid and you'll know whether you get paid monthly or semi-monthly. Set up the automated deposits to your savings account soon after your paychecks are deposited. Maybe a day or two after. At the same time, set up all of your other fixed expenditures to be paid automatically at the same time, possibly on the same days. Then whatever funds are left in your account that month, you'll be able to use as you see fit for your discretionary purchases. In setting up automated payments, you'll make sure that all of your fixed expenses are paid. You'll also be safeguarding the amounts you want going into savings, as those amounts will be deposited before you make any discretionary purchases.

As mentioned earlier in this chapter, we suggest that you review all of your expenditures before you set up any budget plan and then determine if there are any areas which you can eliminate or reduce expenditures. Cut out the things which are not adding value to your life.

Chapter 5—Real Estate Tools for Success

Now that you know how to accumulate the funds you'll need to make the down payment on your first rental property, let's expand the picture and talk about some ways you can build a real estate portfolio and the people you'll want to have on your real estate "team" if you have multiple properties.

Strategies for Building a Successful Rental Property Portfolio.

One of the main reasons the real estate rental market is so attractive is because home ownership is dwindling and the percentage of people who are renting is increasing. That's been happening for a couple of decades now, and with the price of homes continuing to rise, that trend probably won't change any time soon. With this in mind, it's a great time to invest in real estate rental properties and establish a portfolio of profitable properties that will leave you financially set for the rest of your life. Here are a number of different ways you can establish your real estate portfolio past your first rental property:

1) **Buy Multi-Family Units.** We've detailed many of the benefits of multi-family units previously in this book. If you want to build your real estate "empire", one of the best ways to do that is to start purchasing multi-family units. Real estate investment newbies often start with owner-occupied multi-family units such as duplexes, triplexes, and quadruplexes; they then graduate to larger multi-family units such as apartment complexes. In owning multiple units at the same location, you'll be able to consolidate your efforts and costs. An owner who has four single family rental homes will obviously have to put in a lot more time, effort, and running around than an owner who

49

owns a quadruplex. So, if you want to start expanding your real estate rental empire, multi-family properties are a great place to start.

2)   The Snowball Method. Warren Buffet is one of the most successful investors of all time and he has had a lot of success using the snowball method of investing. Most of us who live in the northern areas of the US are familiar with how to build a snowball; some of you in the South may never have experienced snow. So, I'll remind you how a snowball is made. You start with a small ball of snow that often fits in your hand. As you roll that snowball along the snow-covered ground, it gathers additional snow and the ball gets bigger and bigger. We've seen instances of people who make snowballs taller than they are.

The same goes with the snowball method of investing. Instead of using the profits from your first rental property to buy new vehicles or to take luxurious vacations, you can use that profit toward the purchase of another property. Many investors use this philosophy (and some of them don't even know it). It's a great way to expand a real estate empire and, if your properties are profitable, you'll surely find that you'll pick up momentum as you go along. And you'll have a much wider selection of properties to choose to invest in as you make more money. You'll be able to graduate from one single family home or a duplex into multiple single family homes or multi-unit properties, including apartment complexes. So, you'll be wise to let the money you make from your rental property investments work for you. Instead of using those profits solely for personal amenities, you'll be wise to use those funds in other investments.

3)   Start with Partnerships. We discussed some of the benefits of partnerships in the section on how to secure the money to buy your first rental property. Partnerships can also work well beyond the first property. As you get more heavily into real estate investment, you may want to "up the ante" on the properties you're investing in.

You're likely to want to invest in larger, more expensive units. Having an investment partner will allow you to do this more quickly and it will also reduce your financial exposure on the property you're investing in. Also, as far as financing goes, you may find that the banks that financed your previous mortgages, may eventually be reluctant to provide additional mortgages because they don't want to "have all of their eggs in one basket".

4)   The C-B-A Strategy. We previously discussed the different classes of real estate. Class A properties are generally the premier properties—new buildings in great areas. Repairs generally not necessary. Class B properties are generally slightly older properties in good areas. Maybe minor repairs necessary. Class C properties are often marginal properties in marginal areas with many minor or even some major repairs required. Many real estate investors who are trying to build a portfolio will start by investing in Class C properties and then work their way up to Class B and then Class A properties. The C properties are less expensive than A properties and they require a lot more work initially. In starting out with C or B properties, you'll quickly get a good education on what it takes to be a successful rental property investor. Then as you accumulate money from these Class C properties, you'll be able to invest in the more expensive Class B or Class A properties. As we say this, you should know that some investors choose to stay mostly in the same class. We know successful investors who stay mostly with Class B properties instead of ever moving to Class A properties because they find the B properties to be more profitable or more plentiful...or they just feel more comfortable in that area. Either way, you get the idea...you have to learn to take baby steps first before you can walk, and you have to learn to walk before you can run.

5)   Mix It Up. One of the keys to having a successful real estate portfolio is to mix it up...have a diversified portfolio. Some investors get stuck in staying with properties that work for them. Maybe they buy only residential properties and no commercial properties. Maybe they buy only Class B properties. Maybe they buy only properties in the same area of town. Although there is certainly something to be said about staying with what works for you, the "if it ain't broke, don't fix it" approach, there's also something to be said for diversification. We know an investor who for years invested only in properties in a major metropolitan area. These were C properties that the investor purchased and renovated. At the time he started purchasing these properties, that area of the city was revitalizing itself. His investments were extremely profitable and he made a conscious decision never to go outside that area with his real estate investments. Flash forward 20 years after his purchase there. The same area of the city that had once been revitalized was on a severe decline. A middle class/ lower middle class area that had once been moderately safe was now crime-ridden, drug-infested, and dangerous. Schools that were once considered good schools were now considered to be sub-par. Restaurants and other businesses that had previously flourished were struggling, some of them shuttered. The investor's investments were in severe decline, all because he had placed all of his eggs in the same basket and opted not to diversify. Again, no one is telling you that you should abandon the real estate investing philosophy that works for you, but, in the long run, you'll do best if you choose to diversify your investments.

Commercial Real Estate, Another Means to Build Your Portfolio

Commercial real estate is a different ballgame than residential real estate. For obvious reasons, commercial real estate is generally more expensive than residential real estate. Unlike residential real estate, where conventional leases are generally one year, commercial leases usually start at three years and go up to 20 years, depending on how much the property has to be customized for the tenant. If you are a real estate rental newbie, it's unlikely that you'll get into commercial real estate investing in a big way, but we'd nevertheless like to give you a brief capsule explanation of the different categories or strategies of commercial real estate investment.

1)   Core Real Estate Investments. Core investments are known as the safest commercial real estate investments.   With a core investment strategy, investors will look for stable properties in stable areas. This means high quality buildings in low vacancy areas. With a core investment strategy, investors are generally looking yield (immediate payoff) over appreciation (long-term payoff). Return on core real estate investments is generally under 10%, but investors are attracted to this strategy because it is a stable and low risk strategy.

2)   Core-Plus Investments. As the name indicates, core-plus investments are similar to core investments, however they generally offer an opportunity to enhance returns through minor renovation or repositioning in the marketplace. These are still stable and appealing properties with a slightly higher degree of risk (possibly including some key leases that are near expiration).

3)   Value-Added Investments. Value-added investments are the most popular strategy for commercial real estate investment. Whereas core investment strategies will normally bring less than 10% return, value-added investments will normally bring 10-15% return. Whereas the goal of a core investment strategy favors yield over appreciation, a value-added investment strategy favors appreciation over yield. In other words, a value-added investor is often OK with not receiving large profits on the property until it is either renovated, repositioned, or sold. A value-added investor is in it for the long haul and will usually hold the assets for at least five to seven years or until they've had time to enhance or reposition the property. The value-added real estate strategy is a higher risk/higher reward strategy.

Lease terms and lease situations are particularly critical with a value-added strategy. For example, let's take an older industrial complex that was built in the 1970s. The complex has 12 tenants, all of whom had five-year leases when they first moved into the complex. 10 of the leases are due to expire within the next 18 months; the other two leases are for newer tenants. The building has three vacancies. Over time, it has become more difficult to lease spaces to tenants as the complex is one of the oldest within what is still a stable area. With this in mind, it looks like this complex offers a great opportunity for renovation or repositioning which would result in higher rents. On the other hand, if most of the tenants had longer times remaining on their leases, it would probably not be a good time to remodel, as you'd be spending significant remodeling dollars on tenants who are already locked into longer-term leases. So, if you're purchasing rental properties with existing tenants, you'll definitely want to take a look at the lease situation for those tenants to make sure that those leases jibe with the plans you have for the property.

4) **Opportunistic.** Investors who use the opportunistic investment strategy are investors who are willing to take the highest risks to achieve the highest rewards. Opportunistic properties include both existing properties and new developments. With the existing properties, those properties usually need significant work. These are normally high vacancy properties that are difficult to lease. These also might be areas that require repurposing or repositioning. As an example, what was once a huge brewery complex dating back to the late 1800s had been vacant for over 10 years after the brewery had been purchased by another brewery and the brewing plants had been consolidated. A group of investors decided to repurpose the main brewhouse as an international market which now has over 30 tenants. Obviously, this was a high risk/high reward situation as the investor group had to pump millions into the repurposing of the building and the complex. But if they are successful in turning their international market into a high-traffic destination, they'll stand to make high rewards for their strategy.

10 People You'll Need on Your Real Estate Dream Team

If you're going to build a successful real estate portfolio, you're going to have to have a "team" of people you can use throughout the process. Being a successful real estate investor requires a lot of different hats. Unlike some other profit ventures, being a "lone wolf" isn't going to work if you're a real estate investor. You're going to need the help and expertise of others in order to be successful. Here are some of the people you'll need on your real estate rental team as you work toward establishing your portfolio.

1)   **Banker.** Hopefully, you'll be able to establish a working relationship with a banker and he or she will come to know what you are looking for in a bank loan. Fast closing? Lower interest rates?

2)   **Mortgage Broker.** You'll want to find someone who is going to work for you to find the types of mortgage that you're looking for. As with most members on your team, you're going to want someone who understands your business, especially if you are purchasing properties on an on-going basis.

3)   **Accountant/Bookkeeper.**   You'll need someone who understands real estate, including local and state real estate laws.

4)   **Real Estate Attorney.** There are plenty of attorneys out there, but it will behoove you to find an attorney who specializes in real estate. For example, if you have a tenant who is not paying, you'll need an attorney who is familiar with state eviction procedures.

5)   **Insurance Agent.** Again, you'll benefit from an agent who is willing to shop for the best policies to fit your needs.

6)   **Appraiser.** A good appraiser can not only give you an accurate valuation of your property, they can also suggest ways in which you can increase the value of your property.

7) **Inspector.** A good inspector can save you tons of money. If they're thorough, they can tell you exactly what repairs will need to be made in a prospective property and how quickly those repairs will have to be made. A good inspector can be worth his or her weight in gold.

8) **Property Manager.** If you own multiple properties or even if you own just one property and don't have the time necessary to accommodate the needs of your tenants, you'll want a good property manager. Good property managers can often mean the difference as to whether your property is rented or vacant, profitable or not profitable.

9) **Real Estate Agent.** As you continue to build your portfolio, you'll hopefully be able to establish a solid working relationship with a real estate agent who understands the kinds of properties you are looking for. If they don't have a good idea as to what you're looking for, they'll waste a lot of your time.

10) **Cleaning Person or Crew.** Are you going to clean a unit every time it goes vacant? Anyone who has ever done that knows that it can be a lot of work. A good cleaning crew can be a valuable asset to your real estate team.

Again, it's important to note that you should assemble a team that you can use on an on-going basis for you real estate rental properties. In doing so, it will be important for you to communicate to these team members exactly what your wishes are and what you're looking for. If you can do that, they'll became assets for you and you won't have to start at square one every time you have a need for their corresponding services. As with any team, if one of your team members is not meeting your expectations, you'll be better served to find someone else to fill their position. Your success as a real estate investor may well lie in the hands of the real estate team you assemble.

Chapter 6—The Rental to Outshine All Others

So, you're the proud owner of your very first rental property. As expected, it's going to need some work before it's rentable and you'll need to come up with a plan to get the property ready to rent. In this chapter, we'll give you a step-by-step plan on how to rehabilitate a property and get it ready to rent. We'll also tell you about some simple improvements you can make to instantly improve the value or marketability of the property.

10 Steps for Rehabbing Your Rental Property

If you're going to rehab your new rental property, you'll need to come up with a practical plan and schedule for what you're going to do and when you're going to do it. Property owners who do not get organized and instead "fly by the seat of their pants" are setting themselves up for major problems in this process. Also, as you embark on the rehabbing process for your property, you should remember that you may have to remain flexible at times. Murphy's law states that if things can go wrong, they will go wrong and you should not be surprised if you have some hiccups or hit some snags during the process. But hopefully by coming up with a detailed and practical plan before the process begins, you'll be able to minimize any potential problems. Here are some steps you can take in the rehabbing process:

1)   **Assess Each Area of the Property.** Hopefully, you'll have done a preliminary assessment before you purchased the property. You'll need to go through each area of the property and determine what needs to be done to a) make the property livable and b) make it more attractive to prospective tenants. This includes a room-by-room

assessment of the interior of the property and also an assessment of the exterior of the property. If you have purchased a home with a detached garage, your assessment should include the garage. Your assessment should also include a review of the landscaping and the overall appearance of the property. In assessing the property, you'll be well served to get additional sets of eyes involved in the process. (It doesn't always take an expert to determine what they like and don't like about a property. Don't hesitate to secure the services of family and friends for this process.) As you list improvements which need to be made to the property, you should categorize those improvements as Must Make or Could Make, or whatever similar category titles work for you. It's important that you prioritize the improvements you want to make, as you may well have limited time or budget in which to make these improvements and you'll need to decide which changes can be placed on the backburner and which changes need to be done before the property is rented.

2)   Make sure you have the funds available to make the changes you want to make. Hopefully you'll have done this before you purchased your property, but before you start doing any renovations, you'll need to make sure you have the funds to do so and then after you get estimates on the different projects involved in rehabbing the property, you'll then establish a budget to determine how much you are willing to spend to make the necessary changes. Again, you should already have an idea of what these changes will cost before you purchase the property. Then after you purchase the property, you can fine tune or itemize any cost estimates and determine where you'll have to cut corners in the rehabbing process.

3)   Shop around. Especially for newbies, you'll have to spend some time shopping around for contractors and materials. Although no one would ever suggest that you should go with the cheapest available, especially when it comes to materials, you'll probably be very surprised at how much material costs and labor costs vary. You may be able to save thousands of dollars by doing a thorough job of shopping for both contractors and materials.

4)   Line up contractors, service providers in advance. As mentioned above, it's OK to shop around for contractors and service providers, especially with your first rental property purchase. You'll want to determine pricing and also make sure you find people that you are comfortable in working with. At the same time, it won't hurt to interview multiple contractors; in the event that you have trouble with one contractor, you could move to the second contractor on the list, if necessary. And, most importantly, don't wait until the last minute to schedule contractors such as plumbers, electricians, painters, landscapers. You should remember that these people are busy working on other projects and you can't expect them to drop everything they're doing to work on your project. A successful contractor often has a busy schedule that is filled weeks, if not months, in advance. Keep this in mind when you are putting together your rehab schedule.

5)   Draw up a realistic calendar. As you plan your rehab project, you'll need to develop a calendar which lists dates for all of the major tasks. You'll probably start by having contractors visit the property to quote costs for their project. At the same time you are showing them what needs to be done, you should ask them about their availability for the project. When can they start? When would they finish? This information will help you establish your calendar. And one word of caution for you as you set up your schedule. Try not to have too much going on at the property at the same time. If you have the plumber, the electrician, the cabinet installers, and the painter all there at the same time, they're likely to get in each other's way and you're likely to experience delays, or possibly even damages.

6)   Track expenses. You should be tracking your expenses throughout the process to make sure you're going to make budget. Nothing worse than getting halfway through a project, only to find out that you've overspent by a lot and you going to have to delay the project until you can come up with more money. You can use an Excel spreadsheet or Quickbooks to track your expenditures throughout the project.   On the plus side, you might find that you are under budget and this might allow you to add some of the bells and whistles you have previously eliminated when you originally did your budget.

7)   Be there. With a rehab project like this, it's going to be important for someone to be there to supervise while the work is going on. If you don't have the time to do that, you should hire or enlist the services of someone that can do that for you. We've heard stories of contractors that have ripped up floors in the wrong rooms, installed cabinets in the wrong rooms, removed the tiles from the wrong bathroom, etc. Yes, we even had a roofer whose people tore off half the shingles from the neighbor's house by mistake. These things happen and they happen often.   So, it will behoove you to have someone there to supervise or answer questions while the work is going on.

8)   Have a Plan B. What happens if one of your contractors gets delayed on another project? What happens if there is a torrential downpour when your landscaper is supposed to plant the new shrubs or the exterior painter is supposed to paint the outside of the house? What happens if one of your contractors is a total bust and you have to secure another contractor to do the job they were supposed to do? Although you can never plan for these possible hiccups, you should know that these things can and will happen. And when they do, you will have to be flexible and you'll have to move to Plan B, sometimes in urgency. (If you don't have a Plan B, you're going to have to come up with one.) This is never an easy or fun part of the process, but how you handle it may well determine if you're going to be good at being a rental real estate property owner. Most successful rental property owners are problem solvers, and many take pride in their ability to adapt as problems arise.

9) **Secure your materials.** Keep your materials in a safe and secure place. Keep them out of the workers' way, so they're not impacting the way the work is being done or they are not a danger to the workers. Keep the materials in a secure place so they won't get damaged by rain or snow or so they won't get stolen.

10) **Determine a sequence.** As you set up a schedule for the rehabbing projects in your new rental property, it's going to be important for you to determine a practical sequence in which projects should be done and materials should be installed. A lot of this is just simple common sense. For example, don't install the new carpeting until the walls are painted, the new appliances are installed, and the laborers are done tracking through the house. Don't install new kitchen or bathroom cabinets until the painting in those rooms has been completed. Have the electricians and plumbers provide their services early in the process, unless there is a reason they should do later.

The Most Important Rehabs for All Rental Properties

In rehabbing your rental property that are a few items that should absolutely be inspected before you lease to a tenant. Some of the items are frequently overlooked; others can have a major impact on your relationship with the tenant and a major impact on your investment.

1) **The Roof.** We've seen instances of people who have purchased rental properties without even inspecting the roof. That's a big mistake. The roof is an essential structural component of any building and you should make sure you have it inspected, ideally before you purchase the property. If you have to add a new roof to your rental property, that's not going to be a petty cash expenditure. You should know the condition of your roof, so you can plan accordingly for any repairs that need to be done. A faulty roof cannot be ignored and you'll be risking the value of your investment if you don't make sure the roof remains in good condition.

2) **Carpeting, Painting.** Common, relatively inexpensive things that are normally included in any rehab project. If you have shabby carpeting or painting, it's likely to impact your ability to lease the property, as it's one of the first things that prospective tenants see.

3) **Windows.** Like roofs, not an inexpensive proposition. From an investment standpoint, you'll want to make sure your property has upgraded windows as it enhances the value of your property. Also, from a tenant standpoint, a good set of windows can help substantially with the insulation of the house and will reduce heating and air conditioning bills.

4) **Electrical.** 200 amp panels recommended, as they are not much more expensive than 100 amp panels.

5) **Heating/Air Conditioning/Vents.** It's a good idea to have these inspected at least once a year, even when the property is occupied. Heating and air conditioning systems are not cheap and you'll want to make sure they are kept in good condition. You can't expect that your tenants will do so. We've heard stories of properties that have had fires because dryer vents were clogged. Routine maintenance can easily prevent major problems.

6) **Furnace.** Along the same lines, you need to keep tabs on the furnace in your property. An average furnace will last 10-15 years and, as you might expect, they are somewhat expensive. You'll be well served if you know what condition your furnace is in and when you might need another, so you can plan accordingly. You'll also want to make sure that you or your tenant is changing filters in your furnace regularly, as clogged furnace filters can do some serious damage.

7) **Sewer system/plumbing.** Make sure you monitor the sewer system in your property. A sewer backup can cause some serious damage to the property. You should certainly have the sewer lines inspected and checked at the outset of any rehab project. And then have them checked regularly, depending on how likely they are to get clogged. For example, someone who owns a home with a lot of trees on the property may find that they have tree roots that clog the sewer pipes regularly. If you know this, you can schedule routine maintenance on a regular basis to prevent any major problems. At the same time you're checking the sewer system, it's probably a good idea to check all the drains and the garbage disposal. If you can make sure these things are clear before your tenant moves in, you may be able to eliminate middle-of-the-night calls informing you of these problems.

8) **Water heaters.** Water heaters are fairly inexpensive. They'll normally last 8 to 12 years, depending on how hard the water is in your area and how good the water heater is. If your water heater is approaching this age, it's probably a good idea to start thinking about a new one.

Home Improvements to Instantly Boost the Value of Your Property

In the previous section, we focused on functional and structural items which are strongly recommended for any rental rehab project. Now let's take a look at some of the "funner" stuff, things you can do to enhance the cosmetic value, the eye appeal, and the ultimate value of your property. You'll note that many of these cosmetic enhancements are not major renovation or expensive projects. With many of these recommendations, you'll find that you can boost the value or appeal of your property without breaking the bank.

1) **Bathroom facelift.** Regardless of how small it is, the bathroom is considered one of the focal points of any home. Bathroom upgrades including re-tiling, re-caulking, replacing or re-glazing tubs or showers, or a new vanity with modern lighting are all things you can do to upgrade your bathrooms. Research shows that bathroom upgrades can add more to the value of a residential property than any other room. The payback on bathroom upgrades is more than double the amount invested in the upgrade.

2) **Landscape redesign.** Another eye appeal project which can add substantial and immediate value to a property. Things such as trimming shrubs and trees, weeding, and adding new plants or bushes can easily add to the value and the curb appeal of a property.

3) **Minor kitchen remodel.** You don't have to spend a fortune to increase the eye appeal of your kitchen. Simple things such as updated appliances, new counter tops, and new cabinet facings can easily increase the appeal of your kitchen. New floor tiles and new wallpaper are also things that can be done inexpensively to enhance your kitchen.

4) **Exterior improvements.** Besides some landscaping enhancements, you can increase the curb appeal of your home with a new paint job, new siding, new trim, or a new front door.

5)   **Bedroom conversion.** Is there a marginal, non-essential room in the house that you can convert to another bedroom? Even if it is a small bedroom, that extra bedroom can add substantially to the value of a home.

All of the above-mentioned renovations can add substantially to the eye appeal of your home, making it easier to rent. As most homes are now viewed online before a potential renter even inquires about them, eye appeal/curb appeal is more important than ever. If you don't have an attractive property, it's going to be difficult to even get potential renters to visit your property. And from a long-term standpoint, these cosmetic enhancements can also add financial value to your home many times over. For each of the five renovations listed above, the lowest expected payback on the investment is in the 90th percentile. This means that with whatever you invest in any of these areas, you should be able to almost double your investment as it adds to the value of your property.

Chapter 7—Managing Your Rental

OK, you're done rehabbing your rental property. Now it's time to rent the property. Some property owners make the mistake of thinking that most of their work is done and most of their problems are over once they've finished preparing their property for rental. That might well be a drastic misassumption. If you aren't renting to the right people, your problems might just be starting and you might be jeopardizing all of the time and money you've already spent on the property. Getting good tenants into your properties is extremely important. Once the property is ready, your ability to get good tenants may well be the key to whether your property is profitable or not. With this in mind, we have some solid recommendations on what you can do to minimize tenant problems.

Finding Great Tenants for Your Rental

1)   Don't discriminate. Before we get into the basics of what you should do to find great tenants, we should caution you not to discriminate. There are federal laws that prohibit discrimination and you'll need to adhere to these regulations when renting your property. We've read numerous stories of landlords who have been sued for their discriminatory practices and you won't want to be one of those people. Settlement amounts for these lawsuits are sometimes more that the value of the property itself, so we certainly implore you not to discriminate in renting your properties.

The Fair Housing Act prohibits discrimination in the following areas:

--Race or color

--Religion

--National origin

--Sex

--Familial status. (You can't discriminate against families with kids.)

--Disability

2) Create a detailed rental application. Leasing a property is serious business and you should not hesitate to use a detailed rental application that will help you gather the information you'll need to determine whether to rent to the applicant or not. Included in the application should be the following items:

a) Personal references. Ask for two or three personal references, preferably non-family references. Then you need to make sure that you follow up with these references before you rent to the applicant. When you are talking to these references, we suggest that one of the questions you ask them if the tenant has told them why they are moving and then make sure that matches what he is telling you.

b) Employment history. This information might tell you something as to how stable the applicant is. If they've done a lot of job switching or there are an unusual number of employment gaps, this might be an indicator that they won't be a stable tenant. And with employment history, you'll probably be well served to check that the history listed on the application is correct. It's not all that unusual for people to fabricate information on rental applications.

c) Previous rental history. It's possible that your applicant won't have any rental history. (i.e.—recent high school or college grad, retired couple who have downsized, etc.) However, if a history is listed, you'll do well to contact the previous landlords. Instead of just confirming residency, you should also ask other questions that might help you in determining whether the applicant will be a good tenant. Those questions might include: Did they pay their rent on time? Were they clean? Respectful to neighbors and staff? Did they leave the unit in good condition when they vacated? Did they give the required notice before moving out? Did any of the neighbors complain about them? Did they require an unusual amount of attention as a tenant? Would you lease to them again?

d) Credit checks. Run a credit check on your prospective tenant and take it seriously. Some landlords set a credit score limit in renting to tenants. A required credit score of 650 is a common requirement. If the candidate seems like a decent candidate, but the credit score isn't what you'd like it to be, you might ask if there is an explanation for the low score. Credit checks will also tell you how much debt the applicant has (see income-to-debt ratio note in the following verify income category), whether he or she has been evicted from a previous property, and whether he or she has any judgments against them.

e) Verify income. It's not unusual for rental applicants to fudge on their stated income, so it will behoove you to take the time to verify their income. Contact their current employer and verify income, length of employment, standing with the company, and attendance record. As a rule of thumb, you'll want to find a tenant whose monthly income is three times the proposed rent amount. There are exceptions to this, of course, such as retired couples who may have limited income, but have nest eggs that can easily accommodate the rent amounts.

When we say that ideally a tenant should have income which is three times his rent amount, we should also harken back to the credit check/credit score, where you should make a note to check the applicant's income-to-debt ratio. For example, you might have one applicant who has an income of $3000 a month; another who has an income of $2500 a month. You might think that the higher-earning candidate is always the better candidate, but that's not always the case.

Maybe the higher-earning candidate has debt payments totaling $1500 a month, while the lower-earning candidate has no debts at all, except for a nominal car payment. In this instance, the lower-earning candidate might be a better candidate, at least from a financial standpoint.

f) Criminal background check. Criminal history is one of the most "lied about" things on job and rental applications. So, we highly recommend that you do a criminal background check on any prospective tenant that you're interested in. Doing a criminal background check yourself can be very time-consuming, so you may want to use a tenant screening company to do this for you.

Use the information you collect to evaluate the tenant realistically. You should obviously have more concerns about a tenant who has had drug-dealing or sexual assault charges than someone who has multiple speeding tickets. Also, pay attention to when the crimes were committed. Is it a 50-year old man who had some drunk driving charges in his 20s and hasn't had anything since? Or has he had more recent offenses? This information may well make a difference as to whether your prospective tenant is a good candidate or not.

A couple of other quick notes about criminal background checks: If you hire a tenant screening company to provide a background check for you, most of these companies will do a federal and statewide record search, a county search, a Department of Corrections search, and a sexual offender database search. Although this is public information, it can be difficult and time-consuming to gather if you haven't done it before; the cost to use a tenant screening company is nominal. (There is no nationwide criminal database, so criminal background checks are not as thorough or as simple as you might thing they would be.) Also, we should mention that some states, including California, prohibit landlords from discriminating against prospective tenants who have committed certain types of crimes. This means that you'll want to become familiar with whatever your local laws are before you rule out a tenant due to criminal history. That being said, certain past criminal history, including domestic assault, drug- or human-trafficking, drug-dealing, etc., are all activities that should raise immediate red flags for landlords.

g) Face-to-face; gut instinct. When you show your property to your prospective tenants, you should make an effort to get to know them. Hopefully, you can use your meeting with them to start to establish a relationship and maybe get a gut feel as to whether they will be a good tenant or not. And don't hesitate to ask them questions which might help you in determining whether they are a good candidate. Any questions should obviously be appropriate and not too personal (you're not conducting an interrogation), but you might be able to secure some information which will be helpful in evaluating the candidate. Here are some questions you might ask an applicant: Why are you looking to move? Where do you live now? Have you ever rented before? Have you ever had a problem with a landlord before? If you are accepted to rent the property, do you have any idea as to how long you might rent it? What do you do for a living? Do you smoke or have pets? Do you think you'll be a good tenant?

You'll note that some of these questions will be the same questions that are asked on your application form. That's OK. You may be surprised to find out that sometimes the answers you get on an application form don't jibe with the answers to the same questions in a face-to-face meeting. If so, that might indicate some red flags.

Also, in starting to establish a relationship with a possible tenant, you'll then find it easier to go back to them if any questions should arise from their credit check, their reference check, their background check, etc. You might be able to determine how forthcoming they will be, for example, if you ask them why their credit score is "iffy". Maybe there is a logical explanation for their credit score. If everything seems to fit, except maybe one thing, don't hesitate to ask the applicant for an explanation...unless you have many other legitimate applicants for the same property. Either way, the bottom line is that you should use your face-to-face interaction with the prospective tenant to get a feel as to whether they'll be a good tenant. Gut instinct won't trump some of the facts you secure regarding your applicant, however it does count for something and it might be the difference-maker in choosing one candidate over another.

And before we leave this topic, we should mention how important it is to keep good tenants once you have them. You can do this by responding promptly to any tenant requests or questions and also by establishing an open line of communication with them. Let them know that you are there to help them with their needs and it won't hurt to ask them occasionally if they are satisfied with the rental or if they have any feedback regarding the property. If you don't know it already, you'll find out soon...good tenants can make your life a whole lot easier and they can make the difference between a profitable property and an unprofitable property.

We encourage to treat your tenants just as if you would treat a valued customer in any other business. We know successful landlords who send birthday cards, holiday cards, and thank you cards to tenants. We also know landlords who have "exit interviews" with tenants who are vacating the property. In doing so, they'll look for feedback regarding the property. The feedback provided may be helpful to the landlord in future endeavors. Either way, you should always remember that the better the relationship you can develop with your tenant, the more likely it will be for them to continue to rent from you. As you're well aware, any time you have to turn over a lease, you're going to have to spend time to find a new tenant and you also make have some vacancy time in which the property is draining your bank account instead of adding to it.

Strategies for Managing Rental Property

It probably won't surprise you when we point out that if you don't manage a property correctly, that property can turn into a nightmare for you. Instead of being the profit center you hope it to be, it can become a giant money pit and leave you wondering why you ever decided to get into rental real estate. Thankfully, there are a number of different ways you can manage a property successfully. Some rental property owners will be successful with a strictly hands-on approach. Other owners will be successful by outsourcing everything. And others will be successful with a mix of hands-on and outsourcing.

Before you get into these different strategies, it's important to explain the three different areas of managing a property. You'll need to focus on these three areas if you want to achieve maximum profit potential with your rental properties.

1)   Manage tenants. As a rental property owner, you or whoever you hire to do so is going to be responsible for managing tenants. The task of managing tenants includes leasing the property (and determining the viability of tenants), collecting rent, and developing/implementing/updating lease agreements. It also involves handling tenant requests (repair requests and information requests) promptly, coordinating move in and move out dates, and, unfortunately, sometimes evictions.

2)   Managing the property for maintenance and inspections. As a landlord you'll also be responsible for the maintenance and the upkeep of the property. With commercial property or multi-unit properties, this may include the responsibilities of arranging for common area maintenance (grass cutting and landscaping, janitorial services (including restrooms), garbage collection, snow removal, heat and running water, roof leaks, etc. Obviously, residential properties will include less responsibility. In some residential renter agreements, tenants may be responsible for their own snow shoveling, lawn mowing, garbage collection, etc. Unfortunately, with maintenance, you usually won't be able to plan in advance. Problems are likely to spring up at the most unlikely of times, and you'll have to make sure that you or whoever you hire to handle these tasks will be available at "the drop of a dime". Also, you should know that you will have to arrange to accommodate inspections of your property. Local inspectors may want to inspect your property to make sure it meets all health and safety codes, including fire codes. Mortgage and insurance companies may want to inspect the property to make sure that the property corresponds with the amounts they are lending or for which they are insuring.

3)   Managing finances. As a rental property owner, it's going to be important for you to keep a constant handle on how much money is coming in and how much is going out. As we've said before, being a rental property owner is not a hobby, and you'll want to make sure that your properties are as profitable as possible. Rental property financial responsibilities include collecting rent from tenants and then making payments to the various parties involved, including mortgage payments, insurance, and taxes. It also may include making utility payments and paying any fees and fines.

As a landlord, you're going to have to pay attention to all three of these areas. Although it is natural for a person to drift toward the tasks they enjoy doing and wander away from those tasks they don't enjoy, you are going to have to make sure that you are not ignoring any of these areas of responsibility. If you do neglect any of these areas, you're likely to pay the consequences and your neglect will most certainly impact the profitability of your property. That being said, some landlords will make it a point to outsource any of the responsibilities they have no interest in doing, as they are aware that they will tend to neglect these areas. Now that we've outlined the different responsibilities of owning a property, it's time to look at three different strategies to use in managing properties.

The Hands-on/Do-it-Yourself Strategy. If you intend to be a hands-on/do-it-yourself landlord, you're going to have to be a person of many different hats. Landlords will opt for the hands-on strategy for a number of reasons, including total control, the ability to keep costs at a minimum, and the ability to identify and solve problems immediately. This is a lot easier for single unit or owner-occupied properties; it's a lot more difficult for commercial or larger multi-unit properties.

The downside of a hands-on management approach is that you may be attempting to do some things that you're really not knowledgeable enough to do. For example, a rental property owner who sets out to do everything involved may have to be an accounting expert, a legal expert, a maintenance expert (roofer, electrician, plumber). It's likely that you are still going to have to outsource some of the responsibilities involved in being a rental property owner, and you shouldn't feel bad about that. It's normal. In being a hands-on owner, you're likely going to have to be available 24/7/365, and, as mentioned above, you're not going to be able to control when problems arise. Some people find this overwhelming and that's why many owners end up outsourcing certain tasks and responsibilities. Other owners soon find that their time can be more valuably spent doing other things and they'll then outsource certain tasks. As an example, maybe you decide to draft your own lease agreement without the assistance or expertise of a real estate attorney. You could in fact find examples on the internet and then draft your own agreement. But you'll also have to make sure you are familiar with local leasing laws and regulations, which are different in individual states. By the time you finish researching rental agreements, you may find out that you would have been better off hiring a real estate attorney. Or maybe you miss one of the local laws in your agreement and find out later that this omission has left an expensive loophole in your agreement. Bottom line is that you'll have to decide which tasks you're capable of performing and which tasks you're willing to take the time to perform. In some instances, you'll decide that you'll want to outsource some of these responsibilities.

As you can see from the above description, a hands-on management approach is mostly suited toward a landlord who either owns a small number of properties, who has a lot of experience managing properties, or who wants total control in managing those properties.

The Mixed Responsibility Strategy. Most landlords, even those on the smaller spectrum, tend to use a mixed responsibility strategy in managing their properties. We touched on some of this above when we described the possible cons of trying to do everything yourself. Are you a legal expert? An accounting expert? A plumber? An electrician? A roofer? What if you get caught up in an expensive legal battle because you tried to draft your own rental agreement and were not aware of important local rules and regulations? What if you miss a key loophole in paying your taxes because you tried to do your own accounting instead of hiring an accounting expert? You get the picture...sometimes we can get into trouble by trying to be all things to all people. We'll be better served to outsource responsibilities that are outside our areas of expertise or interest.

The biggest benefits of using a mixed responsibility strategy are that you'll free up some of your time and you'll also be assured that your protecting your physical and financial assets by using experts. On the negative side, you'll lose some control and you will be relying on others, placing your reputation as a landlord in the hands of others. So, if you are building your rental portfolio, and you're past the stage of owning your first rental property, the mixed responsibility strategy is probably best for you. The average landlord handles some responsibilities himself and farms out other responsibilities to others.

Outsource Management Completely. There are a number of reasons why rental property owners will opt to outsource all management responsibilities. Some owners will do so because they own non-local properties and it's simply not logistically feasible for them to be hands-on property owners. Some owners own so many properties that they can't be involved on a hands-on basis. And finally, some investors have real estate investments as just a part of their total investments and they simply don't have the time to be hands-on managers.

Most of the landlords who outsource management responsibilities will either hire managers for their properties or they will utilize a management company. Managers or management companies should be able to perform or arrange for all of the tasks that are involved in managing the property: securing and screening tenants, arranging for repairs, coordinating move ins and move outs, collecting rents, pursuing delayed rents, evictions, coordinating routine maintenance and long-term maintenance and upgrades. A good manager or management company should obviously have a good working relationship with the owner of the property. It's obvious that mismanagement of any property could result in the demise of that property.

The upside of hiring a manager or a management company for your properties will be that you will free up a lot of your time. You won't be the one getting the phone calls in the middle of the night from tenants telling you their heat isn't working. And, if you do your due diligence in hiring a good manager or a good management company, you'll know that you'll be using experts in managing these properties instead of trying to wear hats that don't fit you.

The downsides of outsourcing everything involve costs and control. Especially if you are a small-time rental property owner, you're going to have to be aware that a manager, management company, or any of the companies you hire to assist with the responsibilities of owning a rental property (attorneys, accountants, plumbers, electricians) are going to cost money. And, the money you pay them will have an influence on your profitability. That being said, not hiring good managers or other experts in their field, may impact your property's ability to be successful in the long term.

12 Must-Know Tips from Rental Property Experts

Although we've included plenty of tips throughout this book on how to manage your rental properties, we have some additional tips to offer or to expand upon:

1)   Use professional photographs to market your property. You can't derive any rental income from your property if you can't rent it. The importance of good photographs is often underestimated in marketing a property. It's no secret that most prospective tenants will want to view the property and the unit before deciding whether they will visit the property. In order not to get ruled out immediately, you'll want to make sure that you are using attractive photos that properly highlight the property. In advertising your property online, show as many photos as possible. Show each room in the property and also the exterior of the property. If the property has any unique features, show closeup photos of those features. On the other hand, try not to highlight outdated features. Do whatever is possible to show a clean and uncluttered property. Remember that when prospective tenants view your property online, they'll likely be comparing against photos of other properties. Some property owners hire professional photographers to use in marketing their properties. In advertising your rental property, you'll want to make sure it stands out from other properties in the same rental category.

2) **Consider allowing pets.** We've all heard horror stories about how a pet can demolish a residence. But then again, some people demolish their residences also. As homeownership is dwindling, you should know that an open pet policy, usually for dogs and cats, might increase the marketability of your property. You can restrict pet occupancy as you see fit (by limiting the number of pets or the size of pets), and you can even seek an additional deposit or an additional rental fee for a pet. Obviously, when you say you allow cats in the unit, you won't want the tenant to have tigers or lions in there. Ha. And many property owners will restrict dog size to medium or small. Great Danes not allowed! If you're having difficulty marketing and renting your property, this might be an option to consider. We know a rental property owner who rents to a lot of baby boomers who have previously owned homes and are downsizing. He does well in allowing pets in his properties, making them available to a lot more prospective tenants.

3) **Install smart locks in your rentals.** If you're not familiar with smart locks, they are electronic devices which allow keyless entry into a property through use of a smartphone. Although there is obviously a cost involved in installing keyless entry, research shows that these costs typically pay for themselves within seven months of the expenditure. As competitive as the rental market can be, time is money when it comes to leasing properties. When a tenant asks you to show a property and you're not able to accommodate them immediately because of schedule conflicts, they may move on to the next property and you may lose that prospective tenant. Or if you are delayed in showing them the property, it's likely that the lease may be delayed. Studies show that properties with smart locks lease 3-7 days faster than properties with traditional locks. Smart locks are not only safer and more convenient for tenants, they also add to the value of the property and they enable self-showings in which the landlord or the manager don't have to be present.

4)   Landscaping/simple updating. Curb appeal/eye appeal are extremely important. There are many inexpensive ways you can make your property more attractive to prospective tenants. Upon visiting your property, any prospective tenant will see the exterior of your home before they see the interior. If they are already "turned off" before they see the inside of the place, you may have already lost your chance to rent the property. Many landscaping changes can be done on a modest budget. These changes will not just increase the marketability of the property, they will also increase the overall value of the property. Same goes for any features in your property that are noticeably outdated. Features such a granite kitchen counter tops, stainless steel kitchen sinks, well-lit bathrooms, and updated appliances can easily increase the marketability of the property without costing you a fortune.

5)   Rental walk-through. Once you have rented the property, it will behoove you are your property manager to do an immediate walk-through with the new tenant. This walk-through will allow you to identify any immediate concerns that the tenant has. It will also allow you to document any possible concerns. It's better to identify these concerns at the outset of the lease, so any required changes can be addressed immediately. Also, it is better to pinpoint any problems at the beginning of the lease instead of at the end. For example, if you missed some carpet stains at the outset of the lease (maybe the guy installing the new water heater had some leakage when he removed the old water heater), those stains should be documented and photographed on the walk-through, so this will not be a point of contention at the end of the lease when the deposit refund comes into question. These things should always be documented, because by the time you hit the end of the lease, you may well have forgotten about these problems until the tenant brings them up again.

6)   Upgrading when the property is vacant. Whenever possible, you should do your upgrading between leases or whenever the property is vacant. Obviously, you won't want to inconvenience your current tenants with upgrades, if those upgrades can wait and are not emergency upgrades. And we should also mention that it is important for you to take the time to reevaluate your property between every tenant and, if the unit needs upgrading or renovation, then you may be able to delay the start date of the new lease while you make the renovations.

7)   Attend to tenant concerns immediately. We mentioned this briefly before, but it's going to be important for you as a landlord to always address tenant concerns and requests immediately. If a tenant thinks that you are lackadaisical concerning their requests, they may get the feeling that you don't care and you're only interested in taking their money at the end of each month. If the tenant requests a repair and you can't get someone there to rectify the problem immediately, keep your client posted on exactly when they might expect the problem to be fixed. Again, a reminder, tenants who feel that a landlord is attentive to their needs are much more likely to extend their leases.

8)   Express appreciation. A landlord/tenant relationship should be a two-way street and you should make a point to tell your tenants how much you appreciate them (if, in fact, you do). Some landlords send birthday cards, holiday cards, or thank you cards to tenants. Other landlords will send handwritten notes telling the appropriate tenants how much they always appreciate their prompt rental payments or how they appreciate how they always keep the property clean and in good condition. Again, a tenant who feels appreciated is more likely to extend the lease.

9)   Require renter's insurance. This is something that often gets overlooked by landlords. You'll do well to require your renter to have renter's insurance and to demand proof of that insurance. You might think that a tenant is the only one who can benefit from his own insurance. Well, you can also benefit. Let's say that the tenant leaves the bathtub faucet running and floods the unit...or they leave the stove on while they are taking a phone call and a fire results. Or, what happens if your tenant totally trashes the unit, far exceeding the security deposit you have for that unit? In these instances, you will be able to benefit from your tenant's insurance.

10)Keep security deposits separate. Speaking of security deposits, please remember that when a tenant makes a security deposit, that's not your money and you will be wise to keep that money separate and in escrow. If you are ever unable to refund the security deposit at the end of the lease, you are likely to be subject to penalties and fines which well exceed the security deposit amounts.

11)Use property management software. One lost receipt can cost you a possible tax deduction. A lost or misplaced lease can cost you months in eviction court proceedings. Technology can help you manage your property. Instead of having misplaced notes or paperwork in multiple areas of your office, you can have it all in one place. You can use technology to keep track of your property listing, to keep track of rental payments and repair requests and history, signed leases, and tenant screenings. It's good to have all this information in the same place. A property management software program can help you do that.

12)Be willing to make concessions and extend lease terms to good tenants. As mentioned before, finding good tenants can be a trying and difficult task. So, once you find a good tenant, you'll want to work hard to keep them. A vacant property is going to cost you money, even if it is only vacant a month. Along the same lines, you'll have to spend additional time in securing a new tenant, who may not be a good tenant like the last one was.

We've previously mentioned the importance of promptly addressing tenant requests and also establishing a good line of communication with your tenants. Another way to keep good tenants is to offer to extend them or to make concessions if they extend their lease. We've known landlords who have had a lot of success in making or offering renewal concessions. Examples of concessions might be a free month's rent with minimum extension of 12 months or more, no rental increase if lease is extended by a specified date, or, if you live in a northern area and a lease is due to expire during the winter season, you might offer to extend the lease at the same rate for just a few months. This will allow your tenant to vacate at a time when the weather is more conducive to a move and it will allow you as the landlord a better time to find a new tenant, when the rental market is more active. Again, open lines of communication with a tenant can make your job as a landlord a lot easier. Keep in touch with your tenant to find out what their intentions are when the lease expires. This will help you from a planning standpoint and it may also help you get a feel for whether your tenant is even open to an extension.

In a similar vein, if rental rates in your market have been decreasing, and your lease rate is now above market rate, offering a free month's rent or even half a month's rent for an extension might increase your chances for an extension and keep your tenant from shopping other properties.

Chapter 8—Precautions

If you're thinking of getting into the real estate rental business, you've most likely heard some tremendous success stories along the way. Those stories may have amplified your interest in the business. That being said, you need to also be aware of the possible pitfalls of the business. Human nature tells us that investors are not as quick to tell horror stories as they are to tell success stories. Any business that has tremendous success also probably has some serious risks. This is the case with the real estate rental business. We would never attempt to put a damper on your interest to enter the industry, but we want to remind you to go into the real estate rental business with your eyes wide open, just as you would within any other business. Here are some common reasons why rental property investors fail:

1)   **Underestimating overall startup capital.** Some investors make the mistake of underestimating what their startup costs will be for a rental property. They'll look at the sell price of the property itself, and then they'll underestimate the costs to renovate that property or the cost to make it marketable. Please know that although the sell price of the property may be the main expense, you'll have to have enough money to make the property marketable. You'll be well served to do the research on renovation costs before you purchase the property. You'll also do well to pad the amounts you estimate, so you have an extra cushion in there for projects you may have overlooked or cost estimates that come in higher than originally quoted.

We always caution rental property investors not to think that their spending stops with the closing on the property. For some property owners, that's when the spending starts. Even if the property you purchase is in good condition, you may have to do some updates to bring your property up to code, especially if you are going from what was an owner-occupied property to a rental property. Many states and municipalities have different regulations for rental properties and you'll be well-served to know what the rules are in your state and municipality. If you don't, you could be in for some expensive surprises.

2)   **Underestimating or not planning for unexpected/emergency repairs.** This is another pitfall that can lead to failure. The furnace you thought had three to five more years in it goes out and you receive a late-night call on a cold evening from your tenant telling you that he now has no heat. You have to contact and hire a heating company immediately to find out what the problem is. The technician you hire tells you that your furnace is shot and you'll have to get a new one. New furnaces are not cheap and you'll have to have access to immediate cash for the new furnace and installation. Either that, or you could face legal action from a disgruntled tenant. You get the picture. If you're going to get involved in the rental property business, you're going to have to have contingency funds or funding to cover unexpected and sometimes substantial emergencies.

3)   **Deadbeat Tenants/Problem Tenants.** OK, you've purchased your first rental property and spent two months rehabbing it and another month securing a tenant for the property. The monthly rent arrives on time each of the first three months, but then you don't receive the rent for the fourth month. You've had a difficult time reaching the tenant and when you finally reach him, he informs you that they've had some family emergencies and he's been unable to come up with the funds for this month's rent. He'll try to get you some money soon, but things aren't looking promising as he was laid off from his job soon after they moved into the rental. Well, you certainly didn't expect that.

Now, you'll quickly have to become familiar with the eviction process. Not only will you be missing the income you expected from the rental, you now might have to hire an attorney to evict the tenant. And how long before you can evict the tenant? States have different laws regarding tenant eviction and some of those laws allow tenants to stay well past their welcome. And then you'll have to spend time marketing and leasing the property again. It might take you 30-60 days past the eviction to lease the property again. You get the picture. You'll need to have contingency funds to account for deadbeat tenants. Yes, you can reduce the chances of a deadbeat tenant by vetting that tenant properly before you lease them the property, but even with that, life happens and you may be presented with tenants who are no longer able to pay their rent.

We heard an interesting story from a first-time rental property investor who decided to rent out his condo after he purchased a new home. He rented his condo to a man and his girlfriend. The tenant was a well-paid attorney at a reputable law firm. The girlfriend, who was not on the lease, had a fledgling modeling career. Rent payments from this tenant were always prompt until they stopped completely five months into the lease. In contacting the tenant, the landlord was told that the man and his girlfriend had had a blowout and the man was now living with a friend of his instead of living in the rental unit. The girlfriend, now apparently the ex-girlfriend, had continued to live in the rental unit after the fight.

The tenant, an attorney, stated that he no longer intended to make payments (even though he had a solid 12-month lease, and he would not be living there. If his ex-girlfriend wanted to pick up the lease, that would be fine with him. Left to fend for himself against a tenant who was an attorney, the landlord knew he was in the middle of a fiasco. He did a surprise inspection on the property and found out that the front door of the condo had extensive damage, probably from someone who attempted to break down a door in a domestic fight. Upon entering the unit, he also found that there were cats in the unit despite that fact that pets were not allowed in the lease agreement. He also noted substantial carpet damage from what looked to be hair dye.

Who woulda thunk it? The landlord had vetted his tenant properly, he had rented to a party who could easily pay the monthly rent and someone who seemed likely to be a tenant who would care for the property. Yet, now here he was, having to file legal proceedings against his attorney tenant. When the landlord contacted the girlfriend, he found that she was between modeling gigs and couldn't pay the entire amount of the rent because her ex was refusing to help her. She offered to pay half the amount of the rent. This was unacceptable to the landlord and he knew that he'd have to hire an attorney to initiate legal proceedings against his tenant. Thankfully, the woman agreed to move out at the end of the month, so he wouldn't have to evict her.

Yes, it's a horror story, but it does have a "happy" ending. Just before the landlord was about to initiate illegal proceedings against his deadbeat attorney tenant, he mentioned the problem to his racquetball buddy, a corporate attorney for the company the landlord worked for. Ironically, the corporate attorney had a close working relationship with the law firm that the deadbeat tenant worked for. The corporate attorney called a partner at the law firm the deadbeat worked for. The same day, the deadbeat attorney delivered a check for the past due amount and all the remaining months on the lease. The landlord later found out that the partner at the law firm of the deadbeat had read the riot act to the deadbeat and told him that if he ever expected to make partner someday, he'd be well-advised not to tarnish the sterling reputation of the law firm. With that said, the deadbeat delivered a large check covering the remaining months of the lease and he also offered to pay for the damaged door and carpeting. Bottom line, this first-time landlord got lucky. It was pure happenstance that his problem was solved as easily as it was. In most instances, the landlord would have been left "holding the bag", never seeing the remaining months owed on the lease.

This story illustrates two possible areas which can cause tenants to fail: tenant non-payment and property damage. Most of you have heard nightmarish stories about rental units which have been left in disarray by tenants. A moneycrashers.com blog told the story of a landlord who rented to a trio of college students. Again, upon non-payment, the landlord did an inspection of the property. He found a large hole in the ceiling separating the second floor from the ground floor. A large fireman's pole had been haphazardly installed to allow the tenants quick access from the upper floor to the bottom floor. The graffiti which now filled the walls of the until was the least of the landlord's concerns.

4) **Evictions.** If you're under the impression that evictions are simple, you've got another thing coming. Evictions can be expensive and time consuming. First, you may find out that the courts are backed up and you may have to wait a while for a court date. Presuming that you win the case and the court approves the eviction notice, you might then have to wait a while for the sheriff or a member of law enforcement to accompany you when you execute the eviction. You may then find that belongings have been left behind. Most state laws will not allow you to discard those belongings for a certain amount of time and you may have to pay to store them. Besides that, it shouldn't surprise anyone that vacated properties are not always left in the best of condition and you may well have to spend a lot of time and effort cleaning the unit or making damage repairs to the unit. And then there's the fact that eviction of a tenant can take up to 90 days or more in some states or municipalities that require multiple steps for eviction. So, you can see how evictions can bring down landlords. In the property rental business, time is money, and the time and money you spend in evicting a tenant can have a significant impact on your property rental business.

5)   **Managing finances.** Anyone who is in the rental property business can tell you that a landlord's finances don't stay constant. You can sit down at the beginning of the year and make projections for your property or properties, but you'll find that your monthly projections are seldomly going to be what you thought they would be. Things will likely be going well if your units are rented, you don't have any vacancies, your tenants are paying on time, and no major repairs are necessary. But what if you have say five units and two of them have vacancies? Are you prepared for that financially? Whether you are experiencing feast or famine with your real estate real business, you'll need to be disciplined in your finances. Even if things are going extremely well, you can't be sure when your property or properties will require major repairs or vacancies. You'll need to account for these down times by accumulating a sufficient contingency fund when times are good. In the above section on evictions, you saw how long an eviction could take. You'll want to make sure you have the funds to "ride out the storm" in the event that happens. Same goes for vacancies and difficulty in renting out a unit; same goes for major repairs. Do you have the cash on hand to replace a furnace if it goes out? These are all things to consider as a landlord.

6)   **Keep your properties safe and in good condition.** If you have a tenant who gets injured on your property, it's likely that you'll get sued. Even if your homeowner's insurance covers your liability, you'll probably still have to hire an attorney to represent you. Even with a homeowner's policy, you'll be expected to keep your property safe and in working order. As a landlord, it will behoove you to know what your local safety codes are and then follow those codes. We've heard stories of landlords who have been sued for large amounts because they weren't following local safety codes, either because they didn't know those codes or because they ignored those codes.

7)   **Taxes.** Don't overlook property taxes. Make sure you understand the impact that property taxes can have on your property and then plan and save accordingly. It shouldn't surprise anyone to find out that property taxes can have a major impact on the bottom line of your business. By knowing these numbers in advance, you should be able to incorporate them in the rental fees to your tenants.

The above cautionary tales are certainly not meant to scare you away from buying rental properties.   Buying and owning rental properties can be a very lucrative business…if done correctly. It's not all fun and games and it should never be considered a hobby. It's serious business and it's not for everyone. But if you're willing to do your homework and work diligently to become a good landlord, you'll have the opportunity to make money in the rental property business.

Good reasons to let go of rental property.

Many rental property investors wonder about when it's a good time to sell the rental property they own.   There are a number of situations which are conducive toward selling your property:

1)   **You can get more than you paid for it.** Your investment strategy will have an impact on whether you should sell a property that has appreciated. If the property has appreciated in value and it's bringing in profits as a rental property, you'll have to decide whether you want to sell it at any given time. Some investors will want to sell the property and cash in their chips while they can; others will prefer the monthly income they obtain from the property and will choose to hang on to the property. It should be noted that if you sell an appreciated property, you'll know exactly what you're getting for that property. If you hang on to it, you won't know if it will appreciate or depreciate in value; you also won't know if it will remain as a steady rental profit center, depending on the area it's in and the inventory of rental properties in that area.

2)   Negative cash flow. The late Kenny Rogers had a song that said, "You gotta know when to hold 'em, know when to fold 'em, know when to walk away, know when to run". Although those lines from his song weren't meant to describe rental properties, those lines certainly apply to rental property. If you have a property that is not making you money, it's probably time to unload it…unless you have absolute indicators that you'll be able to turn it around quickly. Some real estate investors get caught up in the idea that maybe the negative cash flow properties will change in the future or they can't let go of an emotional attachment they have to those properties. We need to remember that one of the main reasons people invest in rental property is to make money. If you have a property that is not making money, then it's probably time to fold and use the money from the sale to invest in something more profitable.

3)   A strong seller's market. If you have a market that has a low inventory of rental properties in your area and a low mortgage rate for buyers, it's a good time to look at the possibility of selling your property. We all know that the real estate economy (and the general economy) is cyclical and you'll be well-served if you sell your property when the factors work to your advantage.

4)   The property no longer fits your plans. Maybe you are near retirement. Maybe you have health issues. Maybe you are tired of all the attention your rental property requires. Owning rental property can be very profitable, but no one will claim that it comes without work. If the property no longer fits your plans, maybe it's time to cash in your chips.

5) **You're in a good situation with capital gains tax.** If you're not sure if you are in a good situation regarding capital gains tax, you should consult with your financial advisor. If you're able to sell your property without a lot of capital gains taxes, you're in a good position to sell.

Five Crucial Exit Strategies for Your Real Estate Investments

What's an exit strategy, you ask? Simply, it is an investment property owner's plan to remove himself or herself from an investment. Many successful real estate investors will have a specific exit plan in place when they enter into an investment. Others will wait to get into the investment and see how it is going and then develop their exit plans. Either way, it's important to develop some kind of exit plan early on in the process, so you can quickly determine when to exit the investment. Investors who don't have exit plans will often hold on to properties too long, possibly costing them thousands of dollars (sometimes ten thousands or hundred thousands of dollars).

Investors will exit properties for a number of reasons. Maybe the time is right to make a max profit on the property. Maybe they want to exit the property and use the profits to purchase higher level properties or investments. Maybe the investor has determined that real property investment just isn't for them. Maybe the investor is retiring or has health problems or a family or financial emergency.

Here are five main exit strategies for real estate investors:

1) **Fix and flip.** Although this strategy doesn't have anything to do with rental property, it deserves mention as a real estate property exit strategy because of the popularity of flipping, in which investors will purchase properties, work quickly to upgrade those properties, and then sell them for a profit.

2)   **Buy and hold.** This strategy has everything to do with rental property investment, as buyers will buy property, sometimes renovate it/sometimes not, and then they will lease the property to renters with the idea of making steady cash flow from the property as they build equity. Hopefully for the investor, the property will appreciate in value at the same time it creates steady cash flow and then the buyer can sell the property at the appropriate time and turn a nice profit.

3)   **Wholesaling.** This is when someone acts as a middleman in a property purchase. They will purchase the property without any intention of occupying the property or rehabbing the property, and then they will turn around and sell it for a profit to an end buyer. This exit strategy is somewhat similar to a fix and flip strategy, however the wholesaler doesn't put any sweat equity into the project (no rehabbing or renovation). Unlike flipping, which can bring huge profits if done correctly, wholesaling generally brings lower profit margins.

4)   **Seller financing.** With this strategy, the seller acts as a bank. In essence, the seller finances the purchase of the property, with the seller and the buyer having a promissory note that includes the agreed-upon interest rate and a payment schedule. From a seller standpoint, the seller gets to continue to derive income from the property to cover the mortgage loan and their return on investment also increases due to the interest rate.

5)   **Rent to own.** With this exit strategy, the property owner will rent the investment property to a tenant, and then after a pre-determined/set period of time, the tenant will be able to purchase the property from the seller. In some cases in a rent to own agreement, a portion of the monthly rental payment will be set aside toward the purchase of the home. This type of agreement allows the seller to continue to derive income from the property and then if the tenant/potential buyer walks away from the property for whatever reason, the seller has still continued to establish equity in the property.

It should be pointed out that there are numerous factors that will determine whether an investor should exit a property. Long-term goals versus short-term goals will often be a factor. Purchase price of the property, value of the property, and condition of the property may also be factors. Supply and demand, profit potential, market conditions, and financing options will also be factors.

Even if an investor has an exit plan at the outset of purchasing a property, those plans can be derailed by numerous factors. If the property depreciates, the investor may want to dump sooner than expected or make wait until the property rebounds. Tenant issues might escalate or delay the sale of a property. The same goes for unexpected major maintenance costs. Poor property management can have a major impact on the profitability of a property and when that property will be sold. And finally, a distinct lack of demand can affect the exit strategy for a property. You can't sell a property for which there's no demand.

Conclusion

Well, if you've read this far, you should now know a lot more than when you started about the opportunities that are available for you in real estate property rentals. You should have a better understanding of what real estate rental investments can do for you and how you can make money from those investments. You'll know that if you can pay attention to all the areas and responsibilities of real estate rental property investment, you'll have a chance to make money, sometimes a lot of money. You'll also know that if you neglect any areas of real estate rental property investment, you'll inhibit your chances for success and possibly even fail.

You now know how to evaluate properties for possible investment and you also know how to evaluate the neighborhoods or areas those properties are in. You know all about the 1% Rule and the formula for making sure that the properties you are investing in are viable. As many of you are first-time investors, you're going to have to determine ways to finance your first property, often times without a lot of available cash. We've told you about house hacking, a great way to break into the real estate rental property business. We also given you other ideas on how to get properties with no money down and other techniques on how to save money you can use for the down payment toward your property.

We've touched briefly on commercial real estate rental property investment, which is generally for investors as they move up the food chain from novice to expert. We told you to "draft" and develop a real estate team to ensure your success as an investor and we've told you who to include on that team.

Rehabbing properties is extremely important with most Class C and some Class B rental properties. We've given you a step-by-step guide on how rehab properties. Along the same lines, you now know what kind of rehab projects are most important for rental properties. And you also know some simple and inexpensive rehab projects you can do to increase the value of the property immediately.

As a landlord, you'll have to decide how you want to manage your property. Will you want to use the hands-on approach, the mixed approach, or the outsource approach? Regardless of which approach you choose, you'll have to do everything possible to secure good tenants for your property. Good tenants can be the lifeblood of any rental property investments; bad tenants can break you.

As most people get into real estate rental to make money, you'll find that you'll be well served if you have an exit plan for the properties you invest in. "Know when to fold 'em", as Kenny Rogers would say. We've outlined the main reasons people exit properties and also the strategies they use in exiting those properties.

In conclusion, owning real estate rental property can be very lucrative financially, if you can focus on all the different areas of the business. If you can do the research to find good properties at a good price, if you can find good tenants and take care of those tenants, if you can manage the properties well, you'll have a great chance to be successful. That being said, owner rental property in not a hobby. It's not easy money; you'll have to pay attention to detail if you're going to succeed. But if you'll utilize many of the tips and techniques offered in this book, you're likely to be successful and well on the way to financial freedom.

With that said, we'll leave you with six words: Wishing you success! Let's get after it!

MINIMALIST BUDGET

Achieve Financial Freedom Smart Money Management Strategies To Budget Your Money Effectively.

Learn Ways To Save, Invest And Eliminate Compulsive Spending

Table of Contents

Introduction

The Minimalist Budget Mindset is a guide to help you save money, spend less and live more efficiently with a minimalist lifestyle.

M0st people approach budgeting with a deflated spirit and they see it as an impossible thing to achieve. They imagine that budgeting will only give them discomfort and strain. Sometimes even without making the effort, they think they are wholly incompatible with budgeting of any kind.

This book will give you a different approach to budgeting. It's truly unfortunate that the idea of living within your means should be experienced as such a deficit. It brings, after all, an abundance of benefits that most are unaware of. You'll soon see what we mean. This book will show you that when you live a minimalist lifestyle and budget accordingly, you can free yourself from the constraints of the modern world. You can say goodbye to financial problems and pervading feelings of denial. No longer will you be overwhelmed by desires that never seem to give you any satisfaction.

A minimalist budget is an approach to self-fulfillment and abundance that might seem counter-intuitive to most. This book will offer the bigger picture of what it means to budget. You will realize there is more to it than money management. You will also learn that when a life budget considers your behavioral, emotional, social and spiritual capital, you will make much better decisions.

We will talk about spending and shopping habits, identify problem areas, explore debt and how you can achieve your financial goals. You will look at ways you can put these principles into place and ensure that you stay motivated and focused. This book emphasizes the concept of minimalism instead of thriftiness. You aren't buying cheaply, you are minimizing the impulse to buy unnecessarily. That's right, even your cheap purchases need to go. They're doing more harm than you think!

If you can create a budget with a better understanding of your relationship with money and how it affects your lifestyle, the changes you apply will be long-lasting and truly authentic.

Minimalism isn't about surviving with less than you need. It's about identifying what you need and fulfilling the need completely without accumulating excess. Having exactly what you need is far from suffering. In fact, the excess in your life is responsible for more suffering than you even realize. Minimalist budgeting is about knowing what you need to have enough, and how best you can use your money to achieve that. When you approach your finances with this mindset, every penny is used efficiently and nothing is wasted.

We live a short life, and material goods and money can provide us with new ways to enjoy our life. They can assist us in moving closer to what we find worthwhile and meaningful. But that doesn't mean that they are worthwhile and meaningful in themselves. How we spend our money is an expression of what we think is crucial and our values, but in no way does it dictate the value or quality of our life. It gives us the illusion of determining our quality of life, and that's the problem. We are measuring happiness and satisfaction by the wrong standards – that's why we never feel we score very high.

How much would you be willing to pay for the calm and peace of mind achieved through living well? How much of your life do you lose when working? When it comes to expenses, do you remember to consider the time you wasted stressing about money? These questions might seem overly philosophical and vague, but they help us get to the root of how we make money, spend it and form a mentality around it. Once we've understood these roots, our efforts to save money will become much easier. We'll develop a more meaningful relationship with money, and this can mean the difference between scraping by and big savings that shape your future.

What will you learn after reading this book? You'll gain a deeper understanding of what makes a long-lasting budget. You will identify crucial and practical saving tips regarding matters of debt, children, cleaning, home, health, clothes, and food. You will also learn how to set realistic goals that match your personal budget. You will learn how to put everything you have learned into practice, come up with your own personal budget and much more.

The longer you cling to your current bad habits, the more difficult it becomes to shift your behavior and thinking. These money-wasting habits take root inside your subconscious and before you know it, it is second nature. To increase the likelihood of succeeding at minimalism and finally make big savings the new norm, it is vital that you start now. Stop wasting time. Stop making excuses. The longer you wait, the longer it is before you finally achieve your goals.

If you want to free yourself from your current financial constraints, then turn the page and read on. The techniques you'll unlock will make lasting, positive changes to your financial standing.

Chapter 1 – The Minimalist Budget Mindset

In recent years, the minimalism trend has become increasingly popular across the United States, particularly among the millennial generation. It has inspired a lot of people to downsize their possessions and live only with what they need. Aside from helping you declutter and destress, adopting a minimalist view of budgeting may also help you achieve financial freedom, releasing you from the shackles of a life lived paycheck to paycheck.

For one to have a minimalist budget, it's crucial to get into a minimalist mindset. It is the mindset of someone who chooses to live a minimalist life and ensure that this mindset becomes the root of all their behavior.

Most people who choose to simplify their life, do so because they begin thinking differently about how they can live a better life. Or perhaps they start to notice the destructive nature of their thoughtless consumerism, leading to a decided effort to make a change.

You need to cultivate the right mindset to ensure that your hard-earned money is spent well. Without the right mindset, the transition into minimalism is a much more difficult endeavor. You will try to resist temptations. You will try to reduce the amount of physical and mental clutter in your life. You will try to look for solutions. But as you try, the inner urges will continue to grow. Without the right mindset, you will find yourself relapsing. Any attempt at minimalism will only have you running back to satisfy your usual desires. This is why mental and emotional preparations are vital.

You may be wary of the idea of unfulfilled desires. This doesn't mean that you should give up on minimalism. In fact, the minimalist budget mindset is not about fighting your desires at all, it's about learning to stop desiring.

When you have cultivated the right mindset, you will realize that it is easy to live a simple life. Your motives will drive you and your actions will fall into place.

The budget mindset is best seen as a reduction of clutter based on your priorities. This doesn't mean you must get rid of or stop buying things that make you happy immediately. Minimization must be done at a reasonable pace. With time, you will begin to only seek out those things that are crucial.

Most people look to cut back on material possessions and objects, but when the minimalist mindset is involved, it applies to relationships and activities as well. After all, many areas of our life can be filled with excess.

Most people don't understand why someone would want to live a life within a minimalist budget. They don't understand how anyone could want to avoid luxuries.

They believe they should live however they want, and that is true. What these people don't understand is that living a minimalist life on a minimalist budget still allows you to do what you want. The things that you want are simply different. Living on a minimalist budget brings many benefits. It's just that most people are not aware of them.

The money mindset encompasses the thoughts and feelings you subconsciously develop toward money from life experiences. Since our thoughts control our actions, developing a negative mindset when it comes to money can create a huge barrier between you and financial health. It can result in stress and anxiety, and it will hinder you from reaching your financial goals.

But developing a negative money mindset doesn't mean you will always feel that way. Read on to learn how you can develop the right mindset to help you achieve your financial goals.

How to dramatically shift your thinking from a negative to positive mindset when it comes to money

Most people know what they're supposed to do when money management is involved – save funds for an emergency, spend less than the money they earn and invest for retirement. But developing other good habits is crucial. Managing money requires discipline and discipline doesn't come automatically; you must learn and teach yourself to abide by your own goals.

Your success in managing money depends on how you think about money. If you want to eliminate financial stress from your life or get better at money management, it's vital that you change how you think about money and develop a positive money mindset. It applies to every aspect of life. You need to make a positive change in everything you do to be successful. This will help you change what and how you talk.

Speaking and thinking more positively will make a huge difference, but it also requires action. It is essential that you change how you've been doing things, and take steps in a new direction for real and lasting change.

During times of hardship, such as after the death or loss of a partner, it can seem challenging to develop a positive mindset about anything. And not just about money. You might experience even more financial difficulties after this loss. Or perhaps you aren't short of money, but you have no knowledge about how to handle your finances, and this makes you nervous about the future.

Stress due to finances can come from anywhere, and it might become worse when grief or trauma are involved.

Fortunately, there are many steps you can take to dramatically shift your mindset from negative to positive, and develop great habits. Here are the steps you can take:

1. Forgive yourself for financial mistakes you've made

You won't find anyone who has never missed a bill or credit card payment. Everyone has spent some of their savings in the spur of the moment. Virtually all adults have made these same mistakes, and that's why you should forgive yourself.

When you forgive yourself for past mistakes, it will set you free. You will make room for a healthy attitude and better practices for saving money. Stop focusing on guilt and start focusing on progress.

2. Know your money mindset

You may think you understand your attitude towards money, but chances are you're not fully aware of how your mindset affects your decision-making. It's recommended that you track the thoughts that cross your mind every time you make a decision concerning money. What type of items do you find yourself reaching for? What problems do you imagine they will solve? What events in your life trigger these desires?

Since we make a lot of these decisions in our lives, you should do this for at least one whole day and examine the results. Look for patterns that give you a clue about your attitude.

Once you come to a better understanding about your mindset, it will be easy to identify habits and beliefs that prevent you from abiding by plans and goals.

3. Don't compare yourself to others

In the age of reality TV, celebrity magazines and social media, it's easy to make comparisons. We compare ourselves to celebrities, friends, family members and even fictional characters on television. You need to quit this bad habit for a few reasons:

• You're comparing what you know about yourself to only what you see of somebody else. What you're comparing yourself to is the best side of someone's life. What you see in the media is carefully curated for the public and in no way reflective of reality.

- You don't know the details of the other people's finances. Some might live a luxurious life, but it's likely many of these people are also paying off credit card debt.

- After comparing yourself to others, you'll be filled with feelings of inadequacy. This will divert attention from your aspirations and finances, slowing further progress.

Therefore, you should create achievable goals, and measure your success this way. Celebrate the wins and keep your goals updated when you achieve them.

4. Create good habits and maintain them

Once you've established realistic goals, it's good to develop the habits that will help you achieve them. If you've never looked at your expenses in detail or created a budget, then perhaps it's time to do so. When you understand how you're spending money, it can be easy to figure out where you can save.

It'll help you create attainable goals which, step by step, will lead you towards success. One effective habit is following a set time to review your finances and check on progress. If you are in a relationship, choose a time that works for both of you and make sure you're both present.

Even if one partner is appointed to be the money manager, ensure that both parties are on the same page and agree to arranged goals to avoid miscommunication. When you have a clear picture of your financial situation, you can discuss how to delegate money.

5. Become a money mindset sponge

One of the easiest ways to build a good money mindset is to surround yourself with people who live by the values you most admire. When you spend time with people that have a good mindset around money, you will actively learn from them, and you will naturally adapt to their qualities over time.

You can also look for free content online as there are a lot of experts that speak on these topics through live streams, podcasts, and YouTube videos. Consider digesting an hour's worth of money mindset content every day.

Taking this simple step will drastically change your perspective and begin eliminating those limiting beliefs that hold you back from achieving your goals. Changing the people that surround you will change your life.

6. Identify your go-to affirmations for daily empowerment

Find five one-liners that you can repeat daily to center yourself, keep you aligned with your financial goals, and inspire you to make leaps towards success.

For instance, if you struggle with the idea that people with money are greedy, then you're likely engaging in subconscious self-sabotage by keeping a low-paying job. The ideal affirmation for you should be a reminder that having money and being a good person are two different things. Keep telling yourself that you'll give back more to the world when you have more money.

If you grew up feeling that money is scarce and that only some people are entitled to it, then you need to remind yourself there's unlimited money and it's coming your way because you deserve it.

Write down powerful affirmations and keep them in places such as your car dashboard, your wallet, on your bathroom mirror or your smartphone lock screen. Keep reading them out loud. It might seem ridiculous at first, but after some time, you'll start to believe them. Repetition will lead to results, and everything you concentrate on will start to manifest into reality.

7. Ditch negative language

Perhaps you've noticed that most people spend a lot of their time complaining. Sometimes it can be the easiest way to bond with someone, break an awkward silence, or get some cheap gratification.

Most negative conversations revolve around four topics: a bad relationship, work complaints, a bad financial situation, or bad health.

If you engage in these conversations often, you need to stop and concentrate on your dreams. You can't have both excuses and the results at the same time. When you allow unrestricted negative ideas to flow out of your mouth, you can fall into a sense of self-pity and self-victimization. These feelings will prevent you from taking powerful action, and hold you back from your goals.

Eliminate negative language from your self-talk and see everything as an opportunity for growth. Positive language might seem cheesy at first, but it leads to positive beliefs that will attract positive outcomes.

8. Get the right mentors

Think about who you take advice from. Is it your partner? Your parents? Your co-workers? While they may have some interesting insights, they're not always the most helpful mentors.

Challenge yourself to seek advice from those who have already achieved the goals you are trying to achieve. This means you need to get clear about what you want. Do you want your business to make more money? Do you want a new job? Do you want to completely pay off your debt? Don't just seek out those who are close to you; seek out those you are most interested in emulating.

Reflect on what you want, seek out those mentors, and prepare to spend a lot of time learning from them.

9. Practice gratitude

Daily gratitude has proven powerful. You can start by writing down three things you are grateful for each day. Check your gratitude journal every time you are overwhelmed or feeling negative about your finances. This will give you a positive boost. Studies have shown that gratitude practices can actually rewire the brain to feel happiness more often. The more happy you are, the less likely you are to give into your bad spending habits.

10. Learn and implement new knowledge

Being educated on financial matters will help you feel confident and in control of the future. Consider finding the right education for yourself. Different approaches work best for different people. Explore and discover the financial education that suits you best.

You will find books, experts, and educational platforms that offer a range of different approaches. Education is crucial to maintaining a positive money mindset.

Free yourself from a Consumerist Mindset

Most of the world's population has a consumerist mindset. It doesn't just refer to the omnipresence of advertising, but everything related to the idea that we must own more stuff to be better, more successful, or happier people. This mindset is pervasive in today's culture.

We must emphasize that this consumerist belief is not based in any truth. Owning less brings more benefits than owning more. Freedom from a consumerist mindset brings:

• **More freedom from comparison** – You'll be liberated from constant comparisons to other people's lives. No longer will your mind be fraught with envy, looking at what other people have versus what you don't. Constant comparisons can make us depressed and unable to enjoy what we have. Without this in our lives, you'll feel far more secure than you ever have before.

• **More time and opportunities to pursue other things** – Most material things fade, spoil, and perish. But joy, love, purpose, and compassion stand eternal. Our lives are better lived pursuing them. Being less preoccupied with possessions offers this opportunity. Once you clear your life of meaningless objects and expenses, you will have a lot more money and energy to focus on what truly makes you happy.

- **Less debt** – Money that would have gone towards buying pointless new things can now be invested in more important areas of your life. Owning less allows you to finally start saving money and pay off debt.

- **Less stress** – Many people don't realize this, but it can be stressful to own things you no longer use or care about. This can be guilt-induced stress or stress from maintaining the object. Sometimes these useless possessions can even get in the way. The more objects we own, the more stuff we have to break, and the more money we have to spend to maintain or repair the object. Less possessions means less stuff to worry about.

- **Reduced symptoms of depression** – There is evidence to show that consumerism can increase the likelihood of depression and make symptoms worse. This is because consumerism convinces us there's a lack or void that needs to be filled with material goods. This can create feelings of depression, especially since this void does not exist, so nothing we do can change the way we feel. By defending ourselves against the forces that try to create this dissatisfaction, we will feel much more fulfilled in our daily lives. This is who we really are without consumerism in our lives.

- **Gratitude and contentment**– The easiest way to feel satisfied is to appreciate what you have. It's only natural that when you have less, you appreciate what you have even more. You are more likely to care for and maintain belongings when you don't have as much to worry about.

Breaking from compulsive consumerism is an important step towards a simplified life. How, then, do we achieve this freedom? What are the required steps to break free? Here is a helpful guide for achieving freedom from a consumerist mindset.

1. Admit it's possible

It's important to break out of the mindset that the way you live now is the only way you can live. Recognize the lifestyle you're used to is only that – the lifestyle you're used to. It is not the lifestyle you need to be happy. A lot of people throughout history adopted a minimalist lifestyle that rejected and overcame consumerism. Find motivation in how these impressive figures did it. This will help you realize that you, too, can find the same success. The journey to victory starts when you admit it's possible.

2.   Adopt a traveler's mentality

When traveling, people only take what they need for that journey. This ensures that we feel freer, lighter and more flexible. We pack the essentials we can't live without and we realize that all excess creates more stress down the road.

The adoption of a traveler's mindset has the same benefits for life as it does for travel. You'll feel less weighed down, and yet you'll still have everything you need. A traveler's mindset will also prevent you from spending money on items that are unnecessary.

3.   Embrace the benefits of owning less

People don't usually think of the benefits of owning less, but there are many. When these practical benefits are articulated, it becomes easy to understand, recognize and desire. As soon the lifestyle change is made, you can expect to feel inundated with minimalism's benefits, including a stronger sense of lightness and freedom. Instead of focusing on the things you're giving up, start thinking about all the new benefits that will enter your life.

4.   Be aware of consumerist tactics

The world will make you believe that the best way to contribute to society is by spending your money. We are swarmed by advertisements every day trying to convince us to buy more and more. Recognizing the consumerist tactics in our world will not make them go away, but they can help you understand when a desire has simply been manufactured by a well-designed advertisement. Many products that are on the market today don't really solve any problem for us. We are convinced we want it because we have been bombarded by images and videos telling us we want it. But think about it this way: if you had never seen the advertisement, would you have really sat at home wishing that the product existed? Probably not. This is a clear sign of a manufactured desire.

5.   Compare down instead of up

When we start comparing our lives to people around us, we lose contentment, joy, and happiness. We begin focusing all our attention on eliminating this difference. That's because we tend to compare upward, only looking at people who have more than us. We must break the consumerism trap by taking notice of those who have less than us. This will help us remain joyful and grateful for what we currently have.

6.   Consider the full cost of what you buy

When we purchase items, we tend to only look at the sticker price. But the number on the tag is not the full cost. What we buy always costs us extra energy, time, and focus. This also includes fixing, maintaining, organizing, cleaning, removing and replacing. Make a habit of considering these expenses before making a purchase. You'll find yourself making wiser and more confident decisions when it comes to money.

7.   Turn off the TV

Corporations spend a huge amount of money on advertising because they know they can make consumers buy their products or services this way. Television is an industry built on the assumption that you can be persuaded to spend money on nearly anything. No one is immune and even if you don't realize it, TV has likely convinced you to buy something you normally wouldn't have. When you reduce the amount of time you spend watching TV, you are less likely to be persuaded to buy items you don't need.

8.   Make gratitude a part of your life

Gratitude helps us to respond positively to our life circumstances and change our attitude during times of stress. Make it part of your life during the hardships, as well as periods of abundance. Start focusing on the blessings and not just your troubles. Studies have shown that gratitude practices increase our sense of happiness.

9.   Practice generosity

Giving helps us to recognize how much we are blessed with and what else we have to offer. It allows us to find fulfillment and purpose in assisting others. When we act generously, we take on a mindset of abundance, and this can assist us in embracing minimalism. When we give to others, we begin to believe subconsciously that we have a lot more to spare.

It's worth noting that generosity leads us to contentment, and not the other way around. We should not wait to be content before acting generously.

10.   Renew your commitment daily

Everywhere we go, we are flooded with advertisements. At times, it can almost feel overwhelming. We must continue to reject these consumerist ideologies and remain strong in the face of destructive excess. For total freedom, we must cultivate self-awareness and recommit ourselves to our goals every day. The best part is, the more we continue to commit ourselves, the easier it becomes. Soon this commitment to a better life becomes your new norm.

Quick Start Action Steps to free yourself from Compulsive Spending once and for all

At some point or another, we've all been caught up in excessive spending and its destructive cycle. Despite our best intentions, sometimes it can be hard to stop impulse purchases. And as soon as we start spending impulsively, it can be challenging to keep our finances on track. Every purchase is on the spur of the moment, and our actions are no longer conscious.

Although not formally recognized by medical research, compulsive spending is a serious issue, and it has been on the rise for the past few years. Your spending becomes compulsive when it's out of control, excessive and results in legal, social, or financial problems. But even if your consequences aren't as extreme, compulsive spending could still be a major issue you need to quit. Do you frequently make purchases that you can't really afford, yet you make them anyway? That is a problem, my friend.

Some people view spending as a confidence booster, as they think that buying new things makes them seem more glamorous and prosperous than they are. And of course, the public is inundated by billboards, print ads, commercials, and other advertisements to entice anyone with a compulsive spending habit. You think this way because big corporations want you to think this way.

To prevent needless purchases, you should know what you are shopping for and stay focused on exactly what it is you've set out to do. This is a sure way to safeguard against overspending.

If your finances are getting out of hand, you can regain some control with this step-by-step plan. Remember, money doesn't have to slip through your fingers!

1.   Get to the root of the problem

Compulsive spenders accumulate a lot of stuff, but that's not the root of the problem. You must consider what you are really buying. Above all, compulsive spending is a response to an emotional problem. We feel some level of unrest or emptiness, and somehow, we have become convinced that a new purchase is the solution.

A person might be dealing with anxiety, depression, anger, or grief. These emotions can trigger spending, which may result in shame, fear, guilt, feelings of inadequacy, doubt, and many others.

You should identify your triggers and attempt to get them under control. It is recommended to seek professional therapy or support groups to help you manage your spending problem.

You should also consider talking to a friend, and sometimes they can be great therapists.

2. Pay in cash

People tend to spend more when they are paying with debit cards and credit cards. It's no wonder why. Charging bills to a piece of plastic can make you feel disconnected from money. It's easier to ignore what the cost means for your financial situation, and this can easily result in overspending.

Spending feels real when you take dollars out from your wallet. Start setting aside a portion of your income expressly for bills and withdrawing the rest in cash.

Chances are that you will not go on a compulsive spending binge since you can understand more acutely that you have a limited amount of money.

3. Give your purchases a score

Give every item you purchase a score based on how necessary it is to you. The more necessary it is, the higher the score. When you look back at your purchases, you'll see how much you can save by removing the unnecessary purchases. By eliminating low-scoring items, you'll be surprised by how much you can save.

Without scoring the items you buy, it can be difficult to know which purchases matter to you the most. Sooner or later you'll run low on money, with an excess of low-scoring items and possibly a lack of the high-scoring things you truly need.

When it comes to scoring items, you must be honest with yourself. Don't give something a higher score just because you really want it. Really consider how necessary it is. Can something else you own perform the same function? Will the quality of your life really suffer without it?

4. Wait at least 20 minutes before buying anything

When you spot an object you want to buy, your body takes over your mind and it can be difficult to think rationally. To avoid the urge to spend, try waiting for at least 20 minutes before making a purchase. Tell yourself that you can only make the purchase the item if you still feel it's necessary once you've walked away from it. After that time, you may realize you don't really want the item and resist the spending urge. When we are no longer faced with the item in question, it's easier for us to say no.

5. Find social connections

Compulsive spenders waste their money on material goods because they are trying to fill the need for human connection with shopping. The truth is, you can never have enough of the things you don't need. That's why you should learn to fill your life with activities and social connections instead. These activities can involve clubs, learning a new skill, charity groups, or sports.

Many people see shopping as the center of their social life, but it does not have to be this way. When you fill your life with new, meaningful experiences, there will be changes in how you spend and improved satisfaction overall.

6. Pay attention to your spending patterns

You need to know where your money is going. Track how you spend for a month and look for a trend. You might be surprised by the amount of money you lose on insignificant activities like lunch out or frequent coffees.

Take note of your necessary expenses and list them as your priorities. These include:

• Shelter and utilities

- Food

- Transportation

- Basic clothing

All this said, your necessities are no reason to splurge. You don't have to buy new clothes every week or go out to dinner every night. Check your monthly expenses so that you can find ways to trim the spending. Do you need that fancy satellite dish when you can stream your favorite shows on the internet? What about the $40 gym membership you haven't used in five months? Questions like this will help you stay on the path to healthy spending.

7.   Spend money with a purpose

After putting together a monthly budget, create a spending plan to go along with it.

If you need concert tickets or new clothes, ensure that you add them to their budget categories after prioritizing your necessities.

You only need to withdraw the cash you need and sort it into labeled envelopes. For instance, if you choose to allocate $200 every month for groceries, set aside $100 after you receive the first paycheck and have it in a groceries envelope. Add the remaining amount when you get the second paycheck.

If your line of work has an unpredictable cash flow, consider creating a budget for irregular income.

You can use a free budgeting app to create your budget in no time. It will help you plan, monitor your debt, track your spending and monitor your saving process.

8.   Shop with a goal

We've all bought things that we didn't plan. You go to the supermarket and all you need is toothpaste and shampoo, but as soon as you walk through the door, you end up filling your basket with stuff you'll probably only use once. A short trip to the store can become expensive when you're a compulsive spender.

No one plans to get sidetracked when they're shopping, but if you often find yourself spending needless amounts of money, consider planning your trip beforehand. As long as you stick to your plan, you won't have to worry about overspending.

9.   Don't spend money on eating out

Changing your spending habits on food is an efficient way to cut down expenses. Many don't realize it, but dining out can get expensive very fast. If you spend $20 on lunch four times a week, it will cost you $80 per week and $320 per month.

Instead of eating out every day, make a meal plan for one week and buy the required groceries at the store. Make sure to bring a list so you only purchase what you intend to use for your home-cooked meals.

Lunchtime offers a perfect opportunity to cut back. Consider bringing lunch to work every day. Make it simple. Prepare meals on Sundays or take about twenty minutes every night to prepare a sandwich.

This doesn't mean you shouldn't treat yourself, it just means you need to stick to your budget. After all, you can still make delicious and cost-effective homemade meals.

10.   Resist sales

We all love a good deal. Retailers understand this well and they know how flashy sales are irresistible to their customers. Sometimes a big sale can even get people to purchase items they don't really want; they just can't resist the deal, no matter how useless what they're buying is.

If you've ever bought something you didn't mean to buy just because it's 30% off, it means you paid 70% more than you intended. That's not saving money at all; you're still spending. It is essential that you start to practice self-discipline when you see a sale at the store. Remind yourself that keeping all your money is far better than saving 30%.

11.   Challenge yourself to achieve new goals

Strengthen your willpower by giving yourself new challenges. For example, try only to purchase your necessities for a month. You'll be surprised by how little you need.

This will also give you a chance to identify what you don't really need. Do you like paying for your monthly gym membership because it helps you stay active? Then keep it. Do you like going to a chiropractor because it keeps your back in good shape? Keep going. If it fits into the budget and is good for you, then keep enjoying it.

Chapter 2 - Start Saving Money

Do you ever wonder where that money goes? Do you earn a lot of money but still live paycheck to paycheck? Do you sometimes look at your savings and feel like you could do better?

If the answer to any of these questions is 'yes,' then you are not alone. You'd be surprised by the number high-income individuals who can't seem to save a penny. They spend with the mindset that there's lots of money to spare. Funnily enough, they end up having none of it to spare. It doesn't matter how much money you have; if you never spend responsibly, your bank balances will be much lower than they should be.

Most people who live paycheck to paycheck blame their finance issues on lifestyle purchases such as entertainment and dining. Most claim their lack of discipline continues to prevent them from achieving their goals. Their money is lost on things that could be avoided with a little extra effort and creativity.

If you want to achieve your financial goals, you must learn more about your spending habits, create foolproof plans to save money, and cultivate self-discipline in the face of temptation. How do you achieve all this? Let's discuss them individually.

Figure out where the heck all your money goes every month

It's good to have a budget, but if you aren't tracking your expenses, you'll lose track of this budget easily, defeating its entire purpose. You'll run the risk of setting unrealistic goals that you never meet. It is only when you discover where your money is going that you have a good idea of what to cut down. Many people are surprised at what they spend the most money on. You may think it's too many subscription services, but what if it's actually the $5 latte you have five days of the week?

This is the cycle that most people fall into. If you want to make a change, tracking your spending is a must. Here is how it works:

Steps to track your expenses

1. Create a budget

You need a budget to track your expenses. Without one, it would be a difficult challenge to work out what the biggest drain on your money is. A budget shows your expected income and all expenses by category.

A budget doesn't control you; you adjust it as you please. It serves as a guide to ensure your money does what you tell it to do.

There are three steps to creating a budget:

- Write down your monthly income.

- Write down your monthly expenses.

a)   Start with shelter, food, transportation, and clothing.

b)   When the necessities are covered, list other expenses like eating out, TV streaming services, savings, gym memberships, etc.

- Ensure that your income minus expenses comes to zero.

2. Record your expenses

Keep a record of your expenses every day. In a small notepad or your phone's Notes app, jot down everything you spend money on, from your morning cup of coffee to that new pair of shoes. If you fail to keep up with what you spend, you'll feel like you're in a fantasy land where money never runs out. This would be great – except it isn't the real world. Money does run out, and when it does, those consequences can hit you hard.

3. Watch those numbers

Make sure that when you note down your expenses, you track how much is left in the category. This way you'll have a better idea of when the cost of something is too high.

If you are married, talk with your partner and ensure you both record all spending that takes place. Make sure to check in with each other before spending. This practice is excellent for igniting great communication and accountability.

Budgets are blown when you fail to track and watch how you spend.

4 Ways to track your expenses

As we've demonstrated, tracking your expenses is a very important practice. There are also many ways that you can do it. Each method comes with its own advantages and disadvantages. Finding which one suits you best can shape your entire experience of budgeting, determining whether this habit becomes a permanent part of your lifestyle or not. Feel free to try each one out to see for yourself.

1. Paper and pencil

Old-school methods are still extremely helpful. Many people prefer to keep track of their budget on paper. The benefit of physical writing is that it requires an active brain. An active brain will remember more clearly what was written down, so all numbers in the budget are always carefully considered. Using ink and paper also means you can use gel pens and other coloring tools that can make your expense-tracking more fun. The bright colors might even make your task feel less daunting.

The downside to this method is that most of us don't keep paper copies anymore. When you receive a receipt, you must hold onto it until the budget is updated. It's also more difficult to make amendments if you discover you recorded something inaccurately.

You'll likely find yourself misplacing receipts. Sometimes you simply forget to ask for one. Sometimes certain purchases don't get written down. Any of these issues can lead to problematic tracking. And if you lose your expense-tracking sheet, it'll be a big drag to start all over.

2. The envelope system

This method involves paying cash in person. You can create special allocations for utilities, mortgage, and retirement. You can make a debit card payment online or send checks for other utilities. But the expenses you pay in person should only be in cash.

At the beginning of the month, place cash in envelopes labeled with the budget lines. Eating out, entertainment and groceries are the three perfect examples. Remember to carry the groceries envelope with you whenever you go to a grocery store. When the envelope is empty, that's when you stop spending. Using this method, your money will essentially be tracking itself.

Well, the truth is, paying in cash can sometimes be inconvenient. Who likes keeping up with coins or counting out bills? Who wants to go inside a gas station to prepay at the register? Plus, with the recent increase in e-commerce, cash payment options aren't always available. However, this is a great way to track your expenses. That's because watching the envelope become empty will inspire a new level of responsibility.

3. Computer spreadsheets

Many people have gone digital and most of them are spreadsheet fanatics. They love discussing spreadsheet perks, and if you don't know what they're talking about, you probably couldn't care less. The reality is, however, that spreadsheets offer plenty of benefits. This includes the ability to customize your budget, use a plethora of templates, and last but not least, all the math is done for you.

Unfortunately, spreadsheet enthusiasts don't always find a fellow spreadsheet enthusiast. It's likely that only one partner will want to use it. Couples should communicate openly about their preferences. You shouldn't let spreadsheets come between a happy marriage.

Another problem with spreadsheets is getting your computer to keep up with the spending. If you fail to log these expenses daily, your budget won't be a budget at all, just a spreadsheet with good but empty intentions. We all have good intentions in the beginning, but they don't accomplish financial goals on their own.

It's probable that you spend a decent amount of time on the computer, so perhaps spreadsheets will work for you. But do you know what else will always be at your side? Your phone. That brings us to the next and best option for tracking expenses.

4.   Budgeting apps

There are a lot of free budgeting apps that will create a budget in just a few minutes. You can easily log in to your phone and enter your expenses the moment they occur. You won't have to go about your day, risking forgetfulness about your budget updates.

That's how convenient a budgeting app is. Some of these apps let you customize your templates to meet your saving and spending goals. The best part is you can sync your budget with your partner's devices and be in constant commerce communication.

No matter the method you choose, make tracking your expenses a habit if you want to achieve your financial goals. If you fail to track your money, you will always be wondering where your money went. But with the right tools and self-discipline, you can achieve financial victories.

11 simple ways to instantly start saving money

You work hard to earn your money, so it should also work hard for you. Intentionality is the key to making your money go the extra mile. Being intentional is how you'll start saving more and spending less each month. When we are intentional with our money, we know where each penny is going. Every time we swipe our credit card or pull a bill out of our wallet, we are aware of why we are doing it and it is not done out of impulse. This, in turn, keeps more of our money in our account.

There are a lot of ways to save money. Where do you start? Start easy. Start quick. Start here. These are 8 simple tips to help you save money every day, week, month, or year. Here they are:

1. Get cheaper alternatives

If you want to save money, reduce what you spend. There are ways to do this so you still get what you need, but at a much smaller cost. For instance, if you love shopping, consider taking advantage of coupons. You can save money by using cash back or coupons from money-saving apps. Many will let you know about the best prices available on certain items. You can download these apps from your favorite stores and there are a lot of ways you can save money by using them. You can check out sales, nab coupons and join reward programs. Just make sure to resist the temptation to shop online.

You can also look for other alternatives by getting used items. Instead of getting a new item, you can get something used but still in good condition at a lower price. When it comes to buying used items, your discretion is required. Some things cannot be bought used like tires and a toothbrush. But if you're looking for a car, books, video games, tools, or pets, then you can save a lot of money by buying gently used items.

If you love exercising and currently pay for a gym membership, consider other means like finding workout videos online. Some people need the human interaction we get at the gym, while others prefer to lose weight without a membership, special class fees, and a personal trainer. If you want to burn calories without incurring huge monthly expenses, consider exercise-streaming services and YouTube videos. Many fitness gurus have realized that we need non-DVD options we can use at home, and they are creating high-quality content that we can enjoy anytime from the comfort of our home.

Aside from these options, you can also consider brewing your own coffee instead of buying it, and you can cook at home instead of paying for meals at a restaurant. If you spend about $5 per day on your favorite barista blend, it would cost you $35 per week and about $150 per month. Instead of this, you can spend just $20 a month brewing your own and you'll save $130. You can put these savings towards greater things like your dream vacation, retirement, a sinking fund, or whatever your goals are financially.

Instead of paying for an expensive form of entertainment, consider free options. How about e-books, audiobooks, physical books, movies, performances or presentations? Where do you get all of this? At a local library, of course. Get a library card now!

Save money and still have fun.

2. Eliminate the things you don't need
You can save a significant amount of money by eliminating goods, subscriptions, and other services that you don't really need. Do you really need different music and TV streaming services? How many subscription magazines or boxes show up in your mail each month? I am not saying you should avoid these services, but if you haven't thought about them in a while, chances are that you're subscribed to services you don't use, read or watch any more. If you want to save some money, cut out any monthly subscriptions that you no longer have use for.

You can also make further eliminations by evaluating your TV choices. If you pay high cable package prices and only end up watching a few channels, then you are not alone. A lot of people are realizing they can save a large amount of money and still watch the shows they want by choosing other options.

Consider Vimeo, YouTube, Amazon Prime Video, Netflix, or Hulu. Consider watching recently aired episodes online. Or try using that library card.

You don't have to return to medieval times where the only entertainment was watching a joust. You just have to trade that cable bill for a cheaper but equally awesome option.

3.   Eliminate expense-increasing practices

Don't wait for expenses to accumulate before making a change. For starters, consider making more energy-efficient life choices. Some of these might require big initial investments, but they pay off in the end. To save on home expenses, turn off the lights when you leave home, buy energy-saving light bulbs, take quick showers and purchase a programmable thermostat.

To save on transportation costs, use public transportation, carpool, or consider biking. These green options will do wonders for your savings as well as the planet.

If you're considering buying a video game console, think twice. Having a console only means you'll want to spend more money on games. This is an expensive purchase that will only lead to even more expensive purchases.

You should also avoid credit cards so you don't find yourself getting into debt. A great first step to getting ahead is to stop getting behind. That sounds logical, doesn't it? Credit cards are easy ways to fall behind. After all, this is how you accumulate debt in the first place. Debt gives us the illusion of ownership. It keeps out the sunshine of true ownership, however, as it's like a grey, hovering cloud of obligation.

Stop using credit cards, and you will start owning for real. Instead of making debt payments, how about make savings? Not only is this an empowering life change, but you'll thank yourself for it later.

Once you've gotten rid of credit cards, consider removing your debit card information from online shops. The quickest way to spend money these days is through the "one-click" feature. This is when websites store your payment information and make purchases far too easy with a single click of a button. When buying is so easy, overspending is extremely likely. Take your time to retrieve your wallet, pull out your debit card, and do the tedious job of entering all the numbers. As you are going about this arduous process, consider whether this purchase is worth it. Imagine yourself making that transaction and how it will affect your budget. If you still think it's a good idea after thinking it through, then go ahead as you intended.

You can also reduce your future expenses by performing a maintenance check on household objects, such as appliances and cars. Most of these things can be very expensive when replacing or repairing, and a monthly routine check can save you from future financial headaches. Have your car cleaned, checked, and fill the air in the tires when needed. Clean out home vents and remember to check any wear and tear on appliances.

Sometimes a simple bolt, washer, screw replacement, or cleaning can keep it running efficiently.

Before you shop, you should always give it some thought. You don't want to incur huge expenses for something you won't use. Always sleep on a huge decision before taking the plunge. Perhaps even, take a few days. Take the time to check on prices, compare their advantages and disadvantages, and perform desire measuring.

What is desire measuring, you ask? You think you want that trendy, weather-proof laptop case the moment you see it. But does the desire reduce with time? Impulse buying can be expensive. Practice patience to avoid running your wallet dry.

4. Spend creatively

If you want to save money and still get what you want, consider creative ways to find a balance. For instance, a date doesn't have to be expensive to be exciting. There's this pervasive myth that spending a lot of money on a date will guarantee you the love of your life. The truth is, money has nothing to do with it. You can fall in love and have fun while still adhering to minimalist practices.

Consider filling a picnic basket with apples, popcorn, chocolate, and an assortment of cheeses. You can also bring home Chinese takeout and eat while you watch your favorite show. Or how about hanging out at the park? There are many ways to enjoy a date without making your bank account suffer. And if your date can't enjoy the simple things in life, is this really someone you want to see permanently? You might find that minimalism opens your eyes to all the shallow and superficial people in your life. Good riddance!

Consider engaging in more outdoor activities for fun. These activities can offer great entertainment and most don't require a lot of money. There are plenty of things about nature to find fascinating. Consider biking, hiking, spiking, backpacking, kayaking, stargazing, corn-mazing, or curtain-raising. Get out, have fun and save up.

5. Sell what you don't need

Clutter can give us the illusion of completion, but it is the furthest thing from it. Clutter is made up of stuff that nobody really needs. It can be a drain on your energy, overwhelming corners, closets, and drawers all over your house. Having clutter in your vicinity can cloud your sense of clarity. Catching sight of overflowing cupboards may make you feel like your mind, too, is overflowing.

You can cash in by selling the items that you don't need. Post about them online, take them to a consignment shop, or have an old-fashioned garage sale. There are also numerous apps that provide an inviting and fun platform for others to purchase second-hand items.

For clothes, try using Vinted, and for all used books, why not hop on Amazon?

Reduce the number of possessions you don't need, create a calmer home environment, and make cash while you do it.

6. Get excited about borrowing instead of buying

Chances are, if there's something you really need temporarily, someone you know already owns it. Perhaps you're going to a black-tie event and you don't own the right kind of blazer. Perhaps you're looking for a new book to read. Before heading to the store and pulling out your wallet, why not ask your friends if they have something you can borrow? There's a high likelihood they have something you can use. This means you have exactly what you need, and you get to save yourself some money and some extra clutter. Borrowing can be exciting! You can make anyone's stuff your stuff temporarily, and you don't need to pay for it. Just make sure to give it back in good condition as soon as you no longer need it.

7. Take advantage of offers and promos

Businesses provide all kinds of offers to their customers. Try to take advantage of these offers and save money this way. For example, when you're at a restaurant, take advantage of the happy hour specials. These days it extends to meals and not just drinks.

You should also consider eating apps. Subscribe for newsletters from your favorite restaurants, and they'll send you promos and coupons. By eating at a lower cost, you'll save money. And consider unsubscribing from stores or restaurants that tend to make you overspend. This requires some awareness of your spending patterns.

Check the bottom of your receipts as certain restaurants may offer discounts if you take a survey. You can make big savings in exchange for some of your time.

You can also hit up weekly ads and BOGOs. Stores with BOGO offers are practically begging you to save some money. Follow this money-saving move: create a meal plan based on your store's sales. Consider stocking up the freezer and pantry for the future. Keep in mind what you bought when making meal plans, for the future.

8.   Make a shopping list and stick to your budget

Begin by planning your meals – decide on what you will eat at dinner, lunch, and breakfast for a whole week. Then make a list of the individual groceries you'll need to make those meals happen, keeping in mind your budget. You may find that purchasing separate ingredients is more cost-effective than buying many premade meals. Regardless of your preference, always stick to the list you make. This will keep you from overspending and forgetting items in your grocery budget.

9.   Always ask for fees to be waived

When signing up for something, there may be some fees that are involved, and we always end up paying it. You'd be surprised how accommodating certain companies can be when you ask for a fee waiver.

In a recent survey conducted, it was found that over half of responders were successful in getting a bank or other financial institution to waive a fee. The most common fees to get waived are overdraft fees, followed closely by late payment fees.

Doing that won't make you rich, but some extra cash from waived fees can still be helpful. Not all companies will agree to this, but it never hurts to ask. Just make sure to explain your situation honestly and you find yourself being met with a compassionate fee waiver.

10.   Skip the cheap stuff for lasting purchases

Buying cheaper items may save you money in the short-term, but if you want long-term savings, avoid them. It's no secret that cheap stuff tends to be lower in quality. What does that mean? Fragile items that are a lot more breakable. Once it breaks, you'll have to replace it. And that means spending yet more money on a replacement. If you continue to buy something cheap, this cycle will only continue. Eventually, you'll find you've spent a large amount of money on a dozen low-quality things, when you could have spent less money on one high-quality thing. To improve your savings, only purchase items that you know will last.

11. Say a permanent 'no' to one-time-use items

If you're only going to use the item once, do not purchase it. This only applies to non-food items, of course. Were you invited to a 20's themed party but you don't have any 20's themed clothes? You're probably thinking you should head to the store right now to buy a whole new outfit, but this is the opposite of what you should do. This will result not only in clutter, but needless money-spending. Do not purchase items you don't see yourself using for the rest of your life. A better option? Borrow the clothes. They'll be free if you borrow them from someone you know, or at the very least, cheaper than something brand new if you find a store that loans what you need.

How to develop self-discipline to stop yourself from overspending

We start off every month with the intention to save money, by only buying the things we need, staying away from sales displays, and watching our spending closely. Despite our best efforts, we may still find ourselves spending more than we wanted. Sometimes it can even feel like money just slips through our fingers.

Don't beat yourself up, this happens to most of us. There are many reasons why we might overspend. Sometimes it's because we aren't aware of our spending habits. Or because we've estimated our income, debt payments, and expenses incorrectly. This leads to the numbers in our bank account dipping lower than they should. Whatever the reason, if you're ready to take control of your money, here are some useful tips you can apply to develop the personal discipline to stop overspending.

1. Know your spending triggers

To develop self-discipline around spending, you must identify the physical and emotional triggers that make you spend. Once you're aware of these triggers, you can begin to eliminate the opportunity and temptation to overspend. Keep in mind:

Time of the day – Do you have more energy during certain periods of the day? If that's the case, shop only when you have more energy. This way, you'll make wise spending choices. After all, we can think much clearly when we're less pressured and more relaxed.

Environment – Are there certain environments that make you feel like spending? Shopping malls, craft fairs, home shows, and holidays are some examples of occasions on which you're likely to spend impulsively.

You can fight the temptation by taking less money with you or avoiding such environments.

Additionally, if you have a favorite store and sometimes you find yourself wandering through the aisles looking for amazing deals, try to limit the number of times you go there. If you simply can't limit your visits, keep your credit card and money safe from yourself, or ask someone you trust to do it for you.

Mood – Different emotional states and moods can change our energetic resources, making us overspend. For instance, if we're anxious, stressed or upset, we may take retail therapy a little too far. Instead of going to the mall, try hitting up the park or the gym. Exercise and fresh air will do wonders for improving your mood.

It is important to identify the moods that result in your bad shopping habits. Once these moods strike, go somewhere your wallet doesn't need to be involved.

Peer pressure – Do you spend more money than you should when you're hanging out with friends? Even our best friends with the best intentions can be a bad influence, especially if they also have bad spending habits. When you can't afford to eat out, shop, or go on holiday, it's okay to decline their invitations. Feel free to be honest since they are likely to understand.

Or instead, suggest plans that won't make you spend more money. You can meet for coffee instead of brunch, explore new hiking trails instead of going to a concert or have a potluck dinner at home instead of eating at a restaurant.

You may not be having fancy dinners or expensive vacations, but you can still enjoy a great social life. On a minimalist budget, your social connections will not be sacrificed.

If you let your friends know you're trying to spend less, they can even help you on your journey, and some of them may want to follow in your footsteps. The most important thing is finding friends who will support you in achieving your financial goals.

Lifestyle – If you're used to a certain lifestyle, it can be difficult to give it up when faced with financial hardship. But if the overspending continues, you'll only end up in worse shape.

Your upbringing may have influenced your lifestyle choices. If you were brought up in a household where money was tight, you might feel the urge to spend more to compensate for the things you didn't get. Conversely, if you grew up in a family where money wasn't an issue, you'll want to maintain the lifestyle you grew up with. This can be financially detrimental if your source of money isn't the same as it used to be.

The easiest way to live within your means is to find cheaper alternatives. You may have to sacrifice a little bit of comfort, but it's better than losing a lot of comfort when your bank account gets in the red. It can be hard to give up certain luxuries, but no one's quality of life is compromised by this. Most luxury items are excessive, and you'll find that 'above average' brands, as opposed to high-end brands, are still extremely satisfying.

2. List your priorities

You need to categorize your monthly expenses into three main categories: wants, needs, and nice-to-have. Include expenses like car payments, rent, groceries, and utilities in the needs category. Items like new clothes or unnecessary gadgets should go under the wants category. Premium cable channels and entertainment should be listed in the nice-to-have category.

You should establish your goals based on this list. Consider casting the goals in positive terms, and not as things you have to live without. If you always spend $5 each day on fast food lunches, try cutting back to two fast-food lunches per week. Consider bringing lunch from home for the other three days. The extra $15 can be put towards one of your other goals. This will help in debt reduction and still satisfy your fast food cravings. This self-discipline can easily turn into a positive, lasting habit.

3. Learn to budget money

Without a plan, you won't stop erratic spending. If we fail to learn how much we take home and how much we spend, we will keep buying what we think we can afford. You will only realize after a month that you've wasted money when your bank account is empty and there's no taking your bad decisions back. To avoid this, learn to budget your money.

Start by adding up all your sources of income and then all your fixed expenses like debt repayments, rent, car payment, etc. The fixed expenses are easier to budget.

When that is done, list your variable expenses like gas, groceries, and entertainment and allocate funds to each category based on how much you've spent in the past.

Seeing how much you spend on clothing, entertainment, and other wants can help you save on what you don't need.

Try testing your budget. Track your spending for a month and compare that to what you've allocated in your budget. Make all necessary changes to your budget in the next month.

4. Track your spending

The little purchases we make can add up to a huge amount. Without tracking them, your regrets will grow, too. Tracking expenses is the key to successful budgeting. It will keep you accountable for every dollar you spend. When you know where your money goes, it helps you make better choices in the future.

Many people start tracking bigger expenses, but it's crucial to pay attention to the smaller purchases as well. Those lunches out, morning lattes, lottery tickets, or magazine purchases can add up to more than you expect. In fact, you'll find that sometimes they can cost more than the bigger expenses, in the long run. This can affect your budget in significant ways.

5. Evaluate yourself honestly

Every month, compare your spending to what you intended to spend. It's a great time to hold yourself accountable. If you tend to overspend for certain categories, it's time to admit these are your problem areas. Stop making excuses for why you lost control and start reflecting on the real reason you've chosen to spend your money this way.

You need to be honest with yourself since the only person who suffers from this lack of discipline is you. Hold yourself to higher standards and know when it's time to get serious with yourself. Whatever the reason for your overspending is, there is most certainly an alternative that both fulfills the same need and is kinder to your wallet. Get creative and think about what these alternatives could be.

6. Spend wisely

Set aside money every month to cover all your required bills and expenses. Whether you set aside money on your computer or physically, make sure this is a habit you get used to. Resist all temptations to spend money on things other than the expenses.

Pay as many or as much of your bills as you can. Paying more towards your credit card bill, for instance, will reduce your owed balance quickly and save money on interest.

You can buy a "want" every two months so you don't feel deprived.

Resist the urge to get a new purse or the latest tech gadget that's all the rage. Instead, put these items on your birthday wish list or for any other holiday you celebrate. You can also set up a money jar for that item, and put change from your purse or pocket into it every evening. If you used a coupon at a store, put the amount you saved into the jar. Try selling unused items online or at a garage sale, and put the money you earned in the savings jar.

You'll be surprised by how easy money adds up without taking anything away from your monthly bills.

7. Pay off expenses

Make it easy to resist impulsive buying. Consider only carrying the cash you have budgeted for. And perhaps allow yourself a low-interest credit card only for when you really need it. Make sure to only use this credit card when it is absolutely necessary. Even a low-interest credit card can cause you significant debt if it is not used wisely.

Use unexpected income – tax refunds, birthday gifts, annual bonuses – to pay off a high-interest credit card or loan. Remind yourself that putting extra money towards your needs lets you make inroads into main expenses and allows you to pay them off sooner.

8. Reward yourself

Reward yourself when you've achieved significant goals. For example, after you've paid off a huge bill or successfully maintained self-discipline for a long period of time.

After renting movies for a whole month, reward yourself with a show at your local theatre. If you've successfully refrained from eating out on the weekends, reward yourself with one dinner out every month. You've saved money and made progress towards more disciplined spending habits. This is something worth celebrating – just make sure the celebration is within budget!

9. Define your motivations

It's crucial to understand what achieving financial security means for you. It could mean having the freedom to do whatever you want. Or perhaps it's travel, spending more time with family, or more time to write a novel.

Here are other examples to consider:

*   Retiring early

*   Having more money for hobbies

*   Starting a non-profit organization

*   Quitting your job and for a passion that offers lower pay or less stability

Whatever your true motivation is, it's crucial that you identify it and keep it in mind when you feel the nudge of spending urges. Try to figure out how else financial self-discipline can assist you in getting there and what the smaller steps to that destination are. Your motivations may also change over time. Make sure you can adapt to these changes.

10.   Ditch the credit cards

When going to the grocery store or the mall, take the amount you think will be enough and leave the credit card at home. Unless you're sure you can pay it off soon, you shouldn't take credit cards with you at all.

This way you'll avoid impulse spending and the risk of getting into any debt. It's easy to make yourself promises in the heat of a shopping spree. Promises such as, "I'll just be more sensible the next couple of weeks and I can easily pay this off." But the next week, you end up saying the same thing, with no change to your behaviour. Eliminate the possibility of this happening and leave that credit card at home.

Having credit card information saved onto your online shopping profile can make it easy to spend impulsively. All it takes you is a click, and you'll be just a few shoes richer and a lot of dollars poorer.

When you delete these credit card numbers, you make it slightly less convenient to purchase needless items.

11.   Set short-term financial goals

Setting attainable, short-term money goals is a perfect way to remain motivated as you change your spending habits. These goals will constantly remind you of the reasons why you are cutting back on expenses. It's important to focus on short-term goals because long-term goals can seem daunting. It'll take a long time before you achieve a long-term goal (hence the word long-term!) and you may feel you're not making progress. Watching your short-term goals get ticked off will motivate you to keep going. Break up your long-term goals into small, achievable steps.

And, it's also crucial to set specific goals. A goal like 'reduce spending on eating out' isn't going to work well because it isn't specific. You need quantifiable goals like 'I will reduce how much I spend on eating out from $150 to $75 a month.' These goals will give you a target to aim for.

Some other short-term goals include:

- Saving 10% of all paychecks in a different account

- Sticking to a cash budget

- Bringing lunch to work for a whole month

Regardless of your goals, it's important you keep them simple, attainable and out in the open to remind yourself daily.

Chapter 3 - Budgeting Strategies and Financial Plans

Budgeting and saving don't work for many people and for obvious reasons. Even when you have a well-laid out plan, spending on nonessentials is far too easy and straying from our goal is a common occurrence.

The basic concept behind budgeting is simple, but it's in the execution where people fail. To save money, all you need to do is not spend it. I mean, how hard can that be? This is what most of us tell ourselves when we try to establish money habits, but something always makes us lose focus.

There are a lot of budgeting strategies. Different strategies work for different people. You won't find a single budgeting strategy that works for everyone. With the right planning, diligence, and perseverance, it's possible to create and maintain an effective budget.

Before implementing a budgeting or financial plan, you need to know your reason for doing so. If you don't, chances are you won't want to create a budget. And even if you do create a budget, you aren't likely to stick to it if you don't know why it exists in the first place. Perhaps you have been reckless with your spending and you want to stop impulse purchases immediately. Or maybe you're on a debt repayment plan. Or perhaps you are good with your money, but you aren't making great headway on your long-term goals. Whatever the reason, start defining why you want to create a budget. This will keep you focused.

You will also have to figure out your priorities. Budgeting isn't all about math and numbers. It's about living the best way you can by improving your relationship with money. It's about finding out what's important to you and then changing your spending habits to meet your goals and values.

If you have money goals, write them down. Concentrate on the top priorities. The most important thing when concentrating on priorities is honesty. If your priorities are dishonest and don't reflect your personal values, you will be conflicted when making crucial decisions. You'll find it hard to stay motivated and on task. Be yourself when it comes to budgeting.

You also have to monitor your outflow. It's important to do this before and after creating a budget. That's because it can be impossible to know how much to allocate towards certain items without knowing how much you spend in a month. There are many apps and services that allow you to separate spending into categories.

You might discover something that will surprise you. You could find that while you feel you don't make enough, you make more than enough to cover all your expenses and still save for an emergency. Knowing where you stand will help you figure out where you want to be. If you learn that you make enough to save every month, you might want to see where you can cut back to start saving on emergency funds.

Now that you know what it takes to implement a budgeting strategy, we can take a deeper look.

4 powerful budgeting strategies to align your spending with your money-saving goals

There are a lot of ways you can approach budgeting. Some are very simple, while others are more complex and detailed. No method is better than the other. You just have to find a method that fits with your goals and personality. It's vital that you examine each one to determine which method suits you. The most common ones are:

1. 50/30/20 budgeting rule

With this rule, you spend 50% of your pay on needs like debts, insurance, groceries, utilities, and housing. 30% will go towards the expenses of your personal lifestyle. We can also label these as 'wants.'

These expenses are the most likely to blow your budget out of order, so it's the most important to keep under control. It encompasses the things that you can do without, but make you happy nonetheless.

The remaining 20% of your income goes towards savings. This could be saved for retirement, working towards goals, or putting money into an investment. Use these on saving for a car, dream vacation, your children's college fund, and a house.

So, if you earn $5,000 every month, $2,500 should go towards your needs. $1,500 can be spent for your wants, and the remainder should be saved.

Some needs are obvious, but figuring out if something is a want or a need can be challenging. For example, work clothes would be a need, while trendy clothes to go out in would be classified as wants. You might need a monthly subscription service to back up your digital files to the cloud, but a music streaming service would be a want.

It is vital to categorize your needs and wants accordingly to stay on track.

2. Zero-sum budget

In this budget strategy, every dollar you make is assigned a job. The amount of money you make minus your expenses should come to zero.

So, if your total income is $5,000 per month, find a place where that money will go. You should break up your budget into different categories. Consider car-related expenses, eating out, rent and utilities, personal items, groceries, debt, and insurance. If you've covered all your expenses and still have $500 left, you need to assign a task to those remaining dollars.

The value of this budgeting strategy is that it leaves nothing without a task. Every dollar is accounted for and used the way you want.

The best way you can approach a zero-sum budget is by writing it all down. Find out your anticipated income before the start of the month, then create a budget in which those dollars will go and make required adjustments as you progress.

3.   Anti-budget

Contrary to what the name of this budget strategy suggests, it is still a spending plan of sorts. In this strategy, you won't have to worry about putting your expenses in specific categories. You pay as you go. The only catch is you must pay for your priorities first. You immediately pay all your necessary bills, such as rent and utilities, put a small portion in your retirement fund, and another portion in your savings account (we advise saving at least 20% of your income) and *voila!* You can spend the rest however you like. No tedious writing or flicking aimlessly through your bank statements.

This budgeting strategy is perfect for those who want to budget but have trouble starting. This requires consistency and an understanding of your priorities.

Define your priorities and make needs a priority before considering wants. Spend what you have on the necessities, then when all is paid, you can spend the rest on wants.

4.   Money flow budgeting

With this budgeting strategy, some trial and error is required.

When you have figured out how much you need each month to pay for all expenses, you can create a money flow. How does that work? The best way is to figure out what all your recurring expenses are and set up auto-pay for each of them. This includes fixed necessities such as utilities and rent. You will be paying off these expenses directly from your checking account. After money flows in on payday, your bills are paid as soon as they are due. You won't have to touch anything.

This budgeting strategy is best for those who want to forget about when bills are due. You must be comfortable with bill pay automation and of course, you must make the effort to arrange for this in the beginning.

When all the fixed expenses have been paid, take the rest of your income and make a budget. That means that you'll only monitor discretional and variable spending. This includes gas for the car, entertainment, groceries, etc. If you feel like it, you can also move this money into a separate debit card or bank account.

Better yet, if self-monitoring works well for you, you can use a credit card to manage variable expenses. Just make sure to pay the balance in full as the month ends.

You will still have to review your spending regularly and make changes if you feel you aren't making progress. The ideal outcome from this strategy is you'll do less monthly work, and be aware of everything that happens with your money. Even if most of the work is automated, it doesn't mean you get to stop paying attention.

One of these strategies will be suitable for you; you just need to discover which one it is. The approach you choose depends on how you work best, how much work you can put, and the details you want to insert into your budget. The most important thing is that you prioritize making a budget.

Making sure that budget strategy implementation is successful

1. Use your budget

A budget is useless if you don't use it. When you have identified a budget strategy that feels right for you, consider trying it out. Personal finance involves a lot of trial and error. Don't worry if you test out a strategy and it doesn't work. Just try another one instead. Your ideal budgeting strategy will depend on your lifestyle and personal taste. It's important that you find the one that works for you.

2. Update your budget regularly

You will always find room for improvement. Make it a habit to review and change your budget at regular intervals to get maximized benefits from your money. Budgeting takes time. Make a budget, live with it, and over time you'll notice what doesn't work, and you can adjust accordingly. Don't be discouraged if your lifestyle doesn't seem to fit the budget you've created. Feel free to tweak certain aspects until it works for you.

There are no rules you can apply to improve your budget. Personal satisfaction should be your guideline. Are you satisfied with your monthly money management? Are you saving what you need? Are you able to adhere to the rules you've assigned? If you aren't, consider why.

3. Use existing habits to create new ones

Consider an established habit and use it to implement a new one. For example, let's say you always drink coffee every morning before heading to work. If you want to be better at checking how much money is left in your budget, connect these two habits in your daily routine. After drinking a cup of coffee, consider using a money app, or logging in to your bank account to check the balance. Checking your balance every time you drink a cup of coffee makes it easy to remember. As soon as you sit down with that cup of coffee, muscle memory will immediately have you examining your finances. Once this becomes part of your daily routine, you'll have total awareness of your financial standing at all times, making it less likely for you to make decisions that negatively impact it. The new habit of checking on your budget is easy to implement when you link it to a habit you are used to. Try it!

15 Easy steps to come up with a financial plan that lets you save more and earn more

A financial plan is a road map to guide you to a better future. It extends beyond just investing and budgeting. A good financial plan will help you navigate major financial milestones.

A financial plan acts as a set of principles or rules by which you live. The rules of your financial plan should help you in the grand scheme of your life. You need to have a flexible financial plan that allows you to adjust course when life gets tough. The core principles might stay the same, but finances can quickly change when you get married, buy a house, have kids, suffer from a disability or illness, get divorced, gear up for retirement or move across the country. A financial plan should act as a compass to get you back on track.

Your financial advisor might help you set up a plan, but most advisors are focused on product sales such as insurance, investments, and mortgages. Chances are they won't ask where you want to be in the next five years. Also, they might not truly understand your long and short-term money needs.

A better option is to work with a fee-only money advisor. They'll look at your financial health and come up with a plan to help you achieve your goals. The only problem is there are few fee-only advisors and a comprehensive plan might set you back thousands of dollars.

Another good idea is to create a basic financial plan. This process will make you think about money in ways you've never considered before.

Here are simple steps to help you create your financial plan:

1. Identify your goals

You must decide precisely what you want from your finances and which strategies will help you accomplish this.

Do you have children that are expected to attend college someday? If so, you need to save money to make that happen.

At what age do you intend to retire? Knowing this will help you figure out your goal and just how much time you have to achieve it.

Do you want to get out of debt completely? If so, add up all your debt, and determine how much you have to pay towards it each month to clear it in a particular amount of time.

You can also work with a financial planner to target the most realistic and worthwhile goals. Sometimes planners will tell their clients what they want to hear, but a good planner will tell clients what they need to hear.

Also, remember that paying your financial planner is a huge waste if you don't use their advice. It would be like going to a doctor and then failing to take the prescribed medication.

When you have established your goals, identify a solid plan.

2.   Setting up a budget

All financial planning requires you to spend less money than you make. Whether your goal is to retire early or pay off your mortgage, you need extra money to make such a goal a reality. That's why you need a budget. You will find that many people skip this step, which is why they never achieve any meaningful financial goals.

A lot of people think that budgets add stress, but most of the time, it does the opposite.

3.   Cutting expenses

Identify the necessary expenses in your budget. These are what you must pay no matter what. Then identify the expenses that are important but that you could live without. These are necessary, can be cut to some degree.

Identify the discretionary expenses. These may be desirable, but they are not necessary. You can completely eliminate these expenses without affecting your survival.

When you have all your expenses in proper categories, it's time to make reductions. Reduce important expenses and eliminate some discretionary expenses.

4.   Eliminate debt

It doesn't make sense to invest and save money when you are paying a lot of interest on the debt you owe.

Getting out of debt requires discipline, but it's possible. If you're in a lot of debt, you must drastically cut spending and increase earnings to pay it off quickly. Include all your debt except the first mortgage on your home.

When you are out of debt, set up systems that will prevent you from going back into debt. This includes setting aside money for big purchases and carrying the right health insurance so you don't take on sudden medical debt.

5.   Build an emergency fund

When you are out of debt, consider building an emergency fund that can cater to your expenses for six months. This cushion will allow you to leave your investments alone during hard times. This should only be used for real emergencies like job loss, to protect retirement savings and investments.

If you must dip into the emergency fund, focus on returning the money as soon as possible. If you have an unstable job, you should consider saving up to cater for expenses for one year should an emergency arise.

If you are creating a financial plan while still paying off debt, set up a smaller emergency fund of about $1,500 or a month's income to help you cover unexpected expenses. This will ensure you get out of debt without adding more debt.

6.   Determine your net worth

Figure out where you are before thinking about where you want to be. Create a net worth statement to get an idea of your financial situation.

Sum up all your assets and subtract the liabilities. What remains is your net worth. Play around with reduced versions of your current expenses. Seeing the final amount just might motivate you to make cut those expenses for real!

7.   Check your cash flow

If you want a strong financial plan, you should understand how much you save and spend. You can use an app or spreadsheet to track the money that comes in from interest, wages, and government benefits, and the money that goes out for debt payments, rent, and utility bills.

Fill your monthly expenses in a column and the annual expenses in a different column. Add up the expenses in both columns and then subtract them from the total net income on a yearly and monthly basis. You will get your cash flow surplus or deficit.

Tracking your cash flow will give you a sense of confidence and control which makes it easier to implement financial changes.

8.   Match your goals to your spending

Since you have identified your goals and determined the cash flow, it's time to compare your goals to your spending. How well do your spending habits mesh with your goals? If you continue with the spending habits that you have now, will you ever reach your goals? If so, how long will it take?

If there's a cash flow deficit, it means you won't meet your goal, so you'll have to reduce certain expenses to ensure there's money left over. If there is a cash surplus, then you can begin allocating money to meet your goals. Make sure that you put your priorities before your non-essentials.

9.   Review your insurance coverage

Many employer plans provide minimal life insurance coverage. Basic calculations will help you determine if it covers enough. You should ensure that your life insurance is enough to pay off the debts you owe. Also, it should cover ten times your income when you have kids below the age of 10, and five times your income if you have kids above 10.

10. Reduce taxes

Most families have a straightforward tax plan and chances are that you already take advantage of the best tax shelters when owning a home or when you contribute to your TFSA, RRSP, and RESP.

But if you are self-employed and rely on rental income, commission income, or significant investment income, you can hire an accountant to assist you on income tax planning.

11. Create an investment policy

A good financial plan should have an investment policy statement that gives advice on how your portfolio should be invested.

When you write down your investment policy on paper, it will help you stay on track with investments when markets become volatile.

You can create a simple policy. For example, stating that you should invest in low cost, widely diversified ETFs or index funds that will be rebalanced annually to maintain 25% Canadian bonds, 25% US equities, 25% Canadian equities, and 25% international equities. The new money will be added to the lowest valued funds for you to buy low.

12. Create a will and keep it updated

Every adult with assets, children and a spouse should have a will. You need an accurate and up-to-date will so that your assets can be distributed the way you want after you have gone.

Financial planning doesn't end when you die. You should make provisions for what might happen to your property when you are gone. If you don't have a will, chances are the survivors will end up in court battling for your assets. Your assets might even end up disappearing.

Make some time and meet with a trusted attorney to come up with a will that distributes your assets according to your wishes.

Create one now and you can make adjustments in the future if your financial situation changes. All that's important is that actions are taken to prevent your assets from being the subject of conflict.

13. Save for retirement

Perhaps you've been saving for retirement, even if it's just a small amount every month. As soon as you get out of debt, your cash flow will increase, allowing you to save more money for retirement.

If you haven't started saving yet, start with an amount that won't hurt your financial situation. Your goal should be to increase your contribution every year.

You can achieve this by directing your future pay increase into the contribution. You can also increase it by redirecting debt payments once you've paid off debt. If you have a strong financial situation, you'll feel confident contributing a huge amount to your retirement plan, like bonus checks and income tax refunds.

14. Save for other goals

There are a lot of other reasons to save money. Saving for a future college education or a new car are perfect examples.

The reason to save for these other goals is so that more money is available for other expenses and so you can avoid getting into debt to pay for them.

It is no use to work hard to get out of debt, only to fall back into it when faced with a big expense.

Many people get stuck in a debt cycle they can never seem to recover from. That's why a good financial plan should include a prevention strategy. This involves saving money for things that will happen in the future.

You can set up an automatic weekly deposit into your savings account. You can save $150 per week instead of $500 per month. Smaller amounts may be more realistic than larger amounts.

15.   Invest and diversify

When you have maxed out the eligibility on your retirement accounts, you can use other tools like annuities, mutual funds, or real estate to increase your investment portfolio.

You should diversify the types of investments you make. If you are careful and consistent with your investments, there will be a point where the investments make more money that you do. This is a great thing to have in place when you retire, especially since this is passive income.

When you are closer to retiring, you might want to change the way you invest. Make safer investments that won't be affected by market changes. This ensures that you have the money you need even if the economy crashes. When you are young, you have enough time for the market to recover. You can get a financial advisor if you need help with this.

Chapter 4 - Get out of debt

Many people have plans to pay off debt and most of them fail because they haven't identified their true motivation. You may start out fully motivated to repay all debt, but it's easy to become discouraged after making it past the initial stages.

If you want to keep your momentum, you need to continually remind yourself of the reasons you need to get out of debt. How will paying off your debt benefit you? What can't you do now that you can when you're debt-free?

If you haven't identified your true motivation, do so now. Your motivation is the reward you're striding towards. Defining it will make you realize just how much you want it, and how hard you're willing to work to achieve it.

Getting out of debt increases your financial security. It is a serious threat to financial security. The amount you spend on debt payments could have been saved for an emergency, retirement, or for your child's college fund. Being debt-free allows you to be financially secure.

Debt also prevents you from saving money for things you enjoy. Unfortunately, this is why people get deeper into debt. They can't afford the things they love so they make payments on credit until they can't borrow any more. Paying off all debt frees you from this vicious cycle and allows you to spend your income on what you enjoy.

Debt can also lead to more stress as you worry about covering debt payments as well as other expenses. A little stress occasionally isn't harmful, but stress all the time can lead to serious health issues like migraines and heart attacks. Becoming debt free can save your life.

What's unfortunate about debt is the more people you owe, the more bills you must keep up with. When you are debt free, you have fewer bills every month. You'll only have to worry about basic expenses like cell phone service, insurance, and utilities.

A debt-free person has a higher credit score. A huge debt, like credit card debt, will have a negative impact on your credit score.

A debt-free person also teaches their children good money habits by example. If you want your kids to stay away from debt, show them the importance of being debt-free and how to live a debt-free life.

Find out what causes debt

Have you ever considered the reason you're in a debt? Have you ever scrutinized these reasons? We all know that debt can lead us to disastrous consequences in our lives. Sometimes it consumes our assets, hurts our relationships, and brings about intense mental stress.

Many people have fallen deep into the black hole of financial debt. While we may know of the obvious reasons why, there are other factors that lead to debt accumulation.

Most people have spent their adult life in debt and there is nothing fun about it, but it doesn't have to define you.

Even though there are effective debt elimination programs like debt settlement and consolidation, we must be aware of the things that lead us to make great financial errors so that we can avoid them.

1. Failing to use money wisely

The first mistake that gets us into debt is overspending. Many people have gotten into financial trouble because they spent more than they could afford. This usually happens when you fail to set up a budget or create one and fail to stick to it.

If you spend more than you earn, you must learn how to cut your expenses. And once you've cut your expenses, it's time to figure out how you can earn more money.

Another way that people fail to use their money wisely is by not getting insurance. This has made many individuals and businesses fall into huge debt. When you have an adequate insurance cover, especially health insurance, you will stay afloat during an emergency.

The same happens to small businesses. If a small business fails to take out general liability insurance or other insurance covers, they could face significant financial loss if an accident occurs or if they are sued. Business insurance is crucial to all businesses for basic protection.

Some people also fail to save for an emergency fund, so they get into huge debt when an emergency strikes. Even saving a small amount of money can make a big difference. Without an emergency fund, it can be hard to recover from an emergency. You'll have to use your savings or pay with credit. This can lead to a large accumulation of debt.

Some people get into a habit of gambling and end up losing a lot of money. Many view gambling as the best kind of entertainment, but it's just a guaranteed way of giving gambling companies your money. As loans are readily available these days, people are addicted to the idea of winning the lottery and becoming rich. Gambling can lead someone to throw their future away as they try to recover the money they have lost.

2. Life uncertainty

Sometimes things happen in our life that we don't expect and they end up causing financial problems. For instance, medical surgeries can be expensive. Medical costs and expenses can sometimes lead people into debt. If someone has gone through major medical surgery, chances are their insurance will not cover the full cost. Sometimes they may not be insured at all. When this happens, they could easily accumulate huge debt. It can be hard to avoid the massive cost of the procedure, but you can still find great hospitals that charge lower than the rest. You don't have to go to a specific hospital unless your insurance requires it.

Another uncertainty is inflation. Most people don't realize how much the cost of living has gone up. Between gas, food, and housing, and other expenses, most people won't receive a pay rise to offset these increases. If they can't cut back on spending, it might lead to more debt. If you leave your money in a regular savings account, your savings might be stripped due to inflation.

Another reason why people get into debt is a change of income. People will struggle to pay bills, and quickly suck up savings or turn to credit cards.

You might also move to a different house and the council tax band may become high. Perhaps your landlord increases your rent. The interest rate on a mortgage could also go up. How will you cope with these changes? This can easily send a person into debt.

Divorce can also present a strain on personal expenses. There are laws that govern what needs to be done with money during a divorce settlement. If one party demands too much, the other one might have to go into debt to pay for an attorney as well as what the other partner wants as part of the settlement.

4. Identity theft

Identity theft occurs when a criminal illegally opens up an account in your name and then runs up a huge amount of debt. The victim will be left with all the debt that someone else accumulated and they must pay for it. Identity theft cases have been on the rise and it could happen to anyone. To prevent such a disaster from happening to you, make sure that you keep all personal information as safe as possible. This includes your social security number and bank account numbers. Do not give this information to anyone unless you are 100% certain you can trust them. Bank officials usually have other ways of confirming your identity if they need to do so over the phone, so never be forthcoming with a caller who claims to be from your bank. In addition to these precautions, make sure to never leave important mail out in plain sight, where others can easily take hold of them.

5. Lack of financial knowledge

A lot of people don't have the financial experience or education required to make wise financial decisions. They may end up relying on credit cards or getting high-interest loans because they don't know what the best thing to do is. They may also fall for the tricks of many financial institutions. Often credit cards will be offered with seemingly fantastic benefits, and unbeknownst to the financially unaware target, the card will come with a myriad of hidden fees and high-interest. To avoid this, always go through the fine print and make sure you understand what it means.

Also, poor budgeting leads to debt. A person with good financial knowledge knows how important a monthly budget is. Without a good budget, you won't be able to track where your money goes. If you keep track of spending for a whole month, you will see exactly where your money goes and what you need to cut. This is where you can learn about unnecessary expenses. Without this, you can easily overspend and accumulate debt.

6. Expanding families

Many married and single people may feel they have a lot of extra money, but once they decide to have kids, that can change. Your expenses shoot up sharply with each child you have, sometimes more than people even expect. Sometimes families may have to forego one income, which can hurt their finances. If you don't have a kid, then you might not understand how day-care services can cost a lot, but it's something you should always keep in mind, if you're thinking of having a child. You'd be surprised by the amount of money that childcare costs. Make sure to consider all the expenses before you make this huge decision.

7. Taxes and high-interest charges

For most people, federal taxes have been flat for years, but state, produce, and local taxes have continued to increase. This means the average person has less spending money. There are taxes everywhere and the more money we make, the more we're taxed.

Many credit card accounts have interest rates that exceed 20%. This can make it impossible to repay debt. Many have fallen deep into debt because of credit cards.

8. Poor investments

People may have good intentions when they start investing but sometimes these investments turn out to be terrible choices and they end up losing money. This is why it's important to have a decent understanding on what you're investing in. Many people make the mistake of investing in things they barely comprehend.

Sometimes investing can be complicated, but it doesn't have to be. You need to be careful when investing or else you could incur major losses that are difficult to recover from. Consider keeping your investments simple or only making big choices when you have a complete understanding or the guidance of an expert.

9. Burying one's head in the sand

Failing to open emails on your doormat, avoiding phone calls from your creditors and ignoring financial issues will see you get into debt quickly.

Perhaps you don't have enough time to deal with your finances or you think that not opening your mail will make the situation go away. Both assumptions are completely wrong. When you fail to deal with the situation, things will just get worse and accumulate. If you are unable to pay a household bill, then call them. Explain to them why you can't pay and discuss plans. Stare that number in the face and come up with a plan for getting it settled.

Ignoring one bill might turn it into debt. Ignoring two bills might turn it into worse debt with added interest charges. You may even start seeing letters from a solicitor or a debt management company. They will start chasing these payments and this will affect your credit score. Fees will soon come as well. You may be taken to court and given a CCJ. Enforcement agents will turn up unannounced and knock on your door. To avoid this, pick up those calls and stop avoiding those letters.

10.   Comparing yourself to others

Spending money because you think you need the same things as others will soon get you into debt. This is especially true if you cannot afford these things. Most people in society want something their neighbors have, but even if they acquire whatever it is they desire, they'll soon find that they hunger for something else. Desire can become a bottomless pit and unfortunately your money source is far from bottomless. Fashion changes every season and the media pushes products to manufacture desires. It doesn't matter what others are doing. Quit comparisons now. The liberation you'll feel will go beyond anything money can buy.

11 practical techniques to help you get out of debt - regardless of the amount

No matter what you are going through, whether you borrowed a loan or maxed out your credit card, it's your obligation to pay it back. Even if you've faced a life-changing experience like an accident, job loss, or an increase in expenses after having a child, debt will not suddenly decide to be kind.

Overspending can happen at any time of the year. Most people try to get out of debt, but life gets tougher and some end up giving up. This shouldn't be the case for you. There are a lot of people who get out of debt every day. Most people do it in a short amount of time.

If you've started a journey towards financial freedom, you should have a plan for how to handle debt. You may be wondering what the point is if you'll be financially free.

Think of that big project you're planning for. Perhaps it's a home renovation, a school or work assignment, or sorting the garage. Some projects are so daunting that we end up putting them off for a while. A lot of people find it impossible to pay off debt because they deal with them in this manner.

They put off answering the phone, opening the mail, or making any kind of reparation because it seems too big a task. They act as if not looking at the problem will make it disappear.

As tempting as it can be to give into stagnation, the best way to tackle a huge project is to break up tasks into smaller achievable steps. This same rule applies to getting out of debt. Here are the techniques that will help you:

1. Pay off more than the minimum

If you have a credit card balance of about $15,000, and you pay a 15% APR, and make a minimum monthly payment of $600, it will take about 13 years to pay it off. That's only if you don't borrow more money in the meantime. This can be a huge challenge.

Whether you have a personal loan, credit card debt, or student loans, the best way to get out of debt soon is to pay more than the minimum monthly payment. When you do so, you'll save on interest while you repay the loan. It will help you pay off the debt sooner. To avoid headaches, ensure that your loan doesn't charge you prepayment penalties before getting started.

If you need help, there are many mobile and online repayment tools that will help you. They will help you track and chart your progress as you try to clear the balances.

2. Use excess cash to pay off debt

Whenever extra money fall into your lap, use it to speed up the debt repayment process. Some good examples of this unexpected money include an inheritance, profits from selling a car, a tax refund, and winnings from a bet. The more money you put towards debt repayment, the faster it will be cleared. Debt repayment doesn't have to take forever. Use the money you get from your annual raise or work bonus to speed things up.

Any time you get an unusual source of income, divert the money and use it wisely. You can even use the money to clear the smallest balance so that you can concentrate on the largest balance. Resist the tendency to see excess cash as money that you can spend on absolutely anything. As soon as you see excess money in your account, imagine how wonderful it will feel to deduct that excess amount from your debt instead. By paying off debt, you're indirectly making that surplus amount even higher! How? Cause paying off debt reduces your interest rate very slightly. You may regret buying another pair of shoes that looks exactly like another pair you own, but no one regrets paying off their debt.

3. Try the debt snowball method

Consider trying the debt snowball method to build momentum and speed up the debt repayment process.

The first step involves listing all your debts and arranging them from the smallest to largest. Whenever you have excess funds, start by repaying the smallest amount on the list. Consider making minimum payments on the larger loans. When the smallest balance has been paid off, start using the excess funds to repay the next smallest debt until you clear that one and so on.

As time goes by, you'll clear the smaller balances, and more money will be available to clear the larger loans. Clearing the smaller balances first means you'll see less loans on your list much sooner.

4.   Get a part-time job

Eliminating debt with the snowball method might speed up the repayment process, but making more money can speed up the process even more.

Most people have a skill or a talent they can monetize. It could be babysitting, cleaning houses, mowing yards, or becoming a virtual assistant. If no talent comes to mind, check sites like Craigslist for one-time gigs that you can do on the weekends or evenings to make some extra cash.

Look for a part-time job in your area with a local retailer who might need seasonal workers to assist when the stores are busy. These part-time jobs can help you make enough money to get out of debt.

There are other seasonal jobs you can get. During springtime, there are a lot of farm and greenhouse jobs that can benefit you.

During the summer, you can try being a tour operator, landscaper or lifeguard. During the fall, there are seasonal jobs at pumpkin patches, haunted house attractions, and for fall harvest.

No matter the time of year, you will always find a temporary job to help with finances. All it takes is a little extra motivation and some creativity.

5.   Make debt repayments as often as you can

This strategy pays off when it comes to taking care of your mortgage. When you make monthly payments, you will end up paying more interest and miss out on taking advantage of time.

Time will keep moving regardless of how you make your payments, so the easiest and least painful strategy to pay your mortgage loans is to accelerate payments

Change your monthly payment frequency to semi-monthly, weekly or bi-weekly. This will depend on how often you get a paycheck. This change will save you money and time. The best strategy to tackle a big project is to break it into smaller steps.

Making frequent payments is also a perfect strategy to pay off your credit card debt. The more often you make payments, even if it's just with extra money, the less likely you are to waste it on something you won't need. If you want to get out of debt, find ways to make payments as often as you can.

6.   Create and live with a bare-bones budget

If you want to get out of debt quickly, you should cut down on expenses as much as possible. You can use a bare-bones budget to help you with this. This strategy involves getting expenses as low as possible and living a simple life for as long as you can.

A bare-bones budget is different for everyone, but it should aim to eliminate all extra expenses like cable television, eating out, or other unnecessary spending.

You should remember that a bare-bones budget is meant to be used temporarily. When you are out of debt, or when you are closer to your goal, you can start adding these extras back into your budget.

Having a budget that tracks your income and expenses is important when it comes to getting out of debt in a short time. The budget will help you gauge your financial status so you can get closer to your goals.

A budget will show you whether you have surplus money, or if you have a deficit.

7.   Try the laddering method

The laddering method involves listing all your debts, starting with debt that has the highest interest rate and ending with low-interest debt.

This method will save you a significant amount of time with continued use. You will be saving the money you would have used for interest when you clear debt with the highest interest. When you choose this strategy, you need to stick with it. Every month, put as much money as you can towards the debt with the highest interest rate, while still paying the required minimums on other cards. When the debt is paid off, divert the excess funds to the second debt with the second highest interest rate and so on. It is important not to close the account when you have paid off the balance. It will damage your credit. Just let the account sit without funds for a while.

If you have small debts that you can easily pay off, then do so. It will bring you tangible progress to get you started. When you have done that, start tackling the card with the highest interest rate.

8. Sell the things you don't need

If you are looking for a way to get some quick cash, consider selling some of your belongings. Most people have a lot of things in their homes that they don't need. These can range from outgrown clothes to finished books. Chances are there is a heap of stuff you've forgotten about that you'll likely never use again. Take a look around your home and rid yourself of the stuff that you forgot existed. Why not sell those items and use the money for something more worthwhile?

If you live in an area that permits an old-fashioned garage sale, then perhaps that will do. It is the easiest and cheapest way to unload unwanted belongings and make money. If that's not an option, consider selling them through an online reseller, consignment shop, or a Facebook yard sale group.

9. Avoid impulse spending

If saving extra money is what's holding you back, consider tracking your expenses for some weeks to know where your money goes. You might be surprised about your spending habits. Most people don't realize how quickly little expenses can add up. Perhaps you love grabbing a newspaper, buying coffee daily, getting takeout instead of making dinner. These can be categorized as impulse buys if they are purchases that seem to happen automatically. You are so sure you can afford this that you don't even think about it. Learn to make each buy intentional and resist the urge to buy impulsively. These spending habits will prevent you from saving enough money to clear your debt.

There are also other habits that cannot be noticed easily, for example, subscriptions to television channels that you never watch, downloading apps and ringtones, buying toys and gifts at a grocery store because it's convenient.

You can get almost everything you want any time at a local supercentre grocery store. If you want to get out of debt, make sure you avoid impulse purchases.

10. Ask for lower interest rates on credit cards and negotiate other bills

If credit card interest rates are high, it can be impossible to make headway on your balance. Consider calling your card issuer and negotiate. You may not know this, but asking for lower interest rates happens a lot. If you have a good history of paying your bills on time, chances are that you'll get a lower interest rate.

Other than credit cards, other bills can be negotiated down or eliminated. Remember the worst answer you can get is no. The less you pay for fixed expenses, the more money you get for debt payment.

If you are not the negotiating type, consider using apps that will review your purchase history. They'll find repeated fees and forgotten subscriptions you might want to cut from your budget.

11. Consider balance transfers

If a credit card company won't change their interest rates, perhaps it's a good idea to consider a balance transfer. There are a lot of balance transfer offers and you can secure a 0% APR for 15 months. However, you might have to pay a balance transfer fee of about 3% for the privilege.

Some cards don't charge a balance transfer fee for the first two months. They also offer a 0% introductory APR on purchases and balance transfers for the first 15 months.

If you have a credit card balance you can feasibly pay off during the time frame, transferring the balance to a card with 0% introductory APR could save you some money on interest while helping you pay down your debt faster.

It can be easy to continue living in debt if you have never faced the reality of the situation you are in. But when disaster hits, you'll gain a painfully new outlook quickly. One can also get sick of living a paycheck-to-paycheck lifestyle, and consider other ways to make ends meet.

No matter the type of debt you are in – whether it's from car loans, student loans, or another type of debt – it's crucial to know you can get out of it. It might not happen in a day, but a debt-free future can be achieved when one create a plan. You will have to stick to the plan for success.

No matter the plan you have, these strategies can help you get out of debt sooner than you thought. The faster you get out of debt, the quicker you can start living a life you've always wanted.

Chapter 5 - Make more with less

Whether you have some reserve in the tank or are living paycheck to paycheck, you're likely considering how to increase your income. How can you earn more money without losing more time in your day?

It's hard to persist when you have financial problems, but what other options do you have? At the end of the day, this comes down to how you use the money you have and your money mindset. There are a lot of benefits to positive thinking, but that alone isn't enough to help you increase your income.

You must act. That's what it takes. But before you act, you need to know what to do. How will you increase your income so you have enough money at the end of the month? First, you will have to learn how to maximize the use of your income, save enough money, and how to invest and build your personal assets.

Learn how to maximize the use of your income

If you find some extra money in your budget, chances are that you'll use it. While it might seem fun to use it on things you have always wanted, that's not a smart thing to do. The wisest thing to do is spend money on whatever can help you and your family.

You don't have to put all your money in a savings account. While it's good to save some money for difficult times, there are a lot of ways to maximize how you use your income. Although these purchases may not be fun to you, they can help you invest in your future. These wise ways to spend your money will help you live a happy life knowing you're using your money responsibly.

1.   Pay off debt

If you want even more money to spend, pay off your debt. It is one of the smartest ways to spend your money. For instance, if you owe

$2000 on a credit card and normally send the creditor $250 per month, why not use the tax return to pay off your debt? Then you'll have an extra $250 every month. While you may have plans for that money, clearing up $250 per month can make a huge difference in your budget.

2. Buy insurance

Insurance is one of those things we hope we never need, but if we have it when we need it, it can make a huge difference. You need to invest in a plan that will help you. For instance, having a health insurance plan helps to ensure that you always get affordable costs, should you get sick. This also applies to life insurance, home insurance, and auto insurance. When you have a good insurance plan, you are better equipped to handle life's unexpected events. When we put our income towards insurance, we make sure we have all we need in the future, should certain events occur.

3. Invest in a retirement plan

Another excellent way to maximize your income is by investing in a retirement plan. This will help you if you don't want to spend the rest of your life working. Consider investing in your future. If offered, consider having a 401(k) at work, and match what your employer contributes. If you want to take a step further, you can open an IRA. You will be required to invest each year, and the amount you pay will depend on your age.

4. Do home improvements

You don't want to buy a new window or roof until you must. However, investing in home improvements can increase your home's value. In some cases, these improvements can lower your electricity expenses. For instance, buying a new refrigerator can significantly reduce your electricity bill. Home improvements can increase the resale value of your home and turn it into an investment instead of a huge expense. Before doing home improvements, make sure to ask an expert what changes will raise the value of your home the most. Some improvements will be worth more than others.

5. Invest in education

It's always a good idea to invest your money in education. You can take a class to learn a new skill for a job, learn a new hobby, or start a new career or degree to help you get a promotion. A small price now could bring bigger earnings in, down the road.

Whatever your reasons are for investing in education, taking classes can be beneficial. Many will agree it's worth the time and money. In some instances, your employer might even reimburse you for the classes you take. Remember to check with your company first. You could also get tax benefits.

6. Attend a conference

Attending a conference is a great investment. You'll get the latest information about your area of expertise to help you be more successful at what you do. You can meet a lot of people and build a great network. If you are self-employed, it's a perfect way to let potential clients know about your services. You'll have access to a bigger pool of likely customers and this will increase your cash inflow.

Can you live on half your income and save the rest? Probably.

How soon could you achieve financial independence, if you could live on half of what you earn and invest the rest?

Probably within six years, and almost certainly less than ten years.

You should note that retirement and financial independence are not just about how much you earn. It's about how much of your expenses you can pay off with the income from your investments.

You can speed up that process in two ways: increase investments and lower your expenses. Well, the good news is that these two goals can be achieved with the same process. It involves living on a percentage of your income and investing the rest to get more passive income.

Consider this challenge: assume that you can live on half your income and eliminate disbelief. What financial moves would you need to get there?

1.   Make two-week's pay your new budget

When creating your monthly budget, you usually take four week's income into account. Occasionally you will get a bonus paycheck, but normally you'll receive paychecks for four weeks.

If you are normally paid biweekly, it means you receive two paychecks in a month. Your challenge would be how you can live on one pay

check. That's after taxes. That's your new budget.

Does it seem impossible? Well, what would happen if you lose your job tomorrow, spent the next six months without a job, and eventually got a job earning about half your income? Would you be out on the street? Would you starve?

No, you'd have to pay down your expenses and move on. That means its 100% possible to live on half your income. All you have to do is make some lifestyle changes.

Your new budget should only be one paycheck's worth of income. Start by writing your fixed monthly expenses. That includes fixed utility bills, car payment, housing, and other expenses. Then write down your variable expenses like gas for your car, usage-based bills, groceries, and others. And finally, write down semi-annual and annual recurring expenses, such as holiday gifts, insurance, accountant costs, etc.

When you have all that, just cut down unnecessary expenses to fit your new budget.

2.   Eliminate or reduce housing costs

For most people, housing is the largest expense, and it's the first expense that you should scrutinize. Lucky for you, there is a way you can do this without moving to a less desirable home.

This involves getting a small multi-unit property, moving into one of the units, and leasing out the remaining units. The renters will contribute to the housing costs by paying you rent directly.

If you don't want to purchase a new home or move, there are still some options for you. You can segment part of your property as an income suite and then lease it out. You can sign a long-term lease agreement.

Or perhaps you can leave the whole separate income suite, and get a housemate. Housemates come with amazing advantages beyond paying rent. They help with house chores, cook meals, pay utility bills, and they can even become close friends.

If none of this sounds doable, then why not consider moving to a smaller home? A minimalist lifestyle will downsize your possessions so you may need less space than you did before. Perhaps even consider moving to a slightly less popular neighbourhood. All of these factors can reduce your rent significantly, and it doesn't necessarily mean your home is any less comfortable or attractive.

3.   Learn to cook

Eating out or paying someone to cook for you can create huge expenses. They are budget killers and let's face it, they're not necessary.

Why don't you learn to cook? With time, you'll get better at it and you may even learn to enjoy it.

Anyone can learn to cook, and once you get over the initial awkwardness, you can learn to complete a three-course meal that beats anything at an overpriced restaurant. It will cost significantly lower prices to cook, and you can make extra food for the next day.

Also, when you cook for yourself, you'll end up cooking healthier meals than anything you'll find at a restaurant. You can pick low-carb or low-fat dishes and ingredients. Restaurants only prioritize taste, meaning excessive salt is often used.

4. Move your social life away from shopping

Where do you normally meet your friends? Bars? Movie theatres? Restaurants?

Since you can now cook, you can invite them over for dinner. You can also take cooler drinks somewhere with an amazing view instead of the bar. Instead of overpaying to get a movie ticket, plan a movie night at your or your friend's home. These days, movies can be rented online for a few dollars, and if you're tech savvy, they can even be streamed for free.

You could spend $100 eating out at a restaurant with friends, or you could spend $20 getting together for a bonfire or a picnic at the beach. Consider other options as well, such as a home wine-tasting or a backyard BBQ.

All it takes is a little more creativity and planning, but it will help you save an enormous amount of money without losing out on fun with friends.

5. Earn more money

If you are struggling to make ends meet with a two-week income, look for other ways to make more money. There are a lot of ways you can deal with this. You could negotiate for a pay rise at your workplace, or you could look for a new job that pays better. Find anything that can make you a more valuable employee and do it. If that's not possible, look for a part-time job to earn extra money.

What skills do you have that others need? Can you build websites on WordPress? Are you good at photography, and willing to work weddings for some weekend evenings every month? Do you have home improvement experience?

We all have skills, and everyone can learn to develop them. There are many ways to earn money, but it requires initiative on your part.

6. Automatically transfer half of your income

You will always be tempted to use money in your operating or checking account.

You can set up an automatic transfer from your account to an investment or savings account. You should do this transfer the same day you are paid.

In the beginning, you can use half of your income to pay off your debts. When all the debts are paid off, your budget will be very easy to deal with. With no debts, you can begin investing in high-yield investments that pay you. You will soon start rising, and you will be in a fantastic cycle where your income keeps on increasing.

That cycle will only take off if you keep expenses low. Most people only go out to spend when they get more money. They want a new car, fancy dinners out, a new house, and new clothes. That's what they call lifestyle inflation, and it's an enemy of financial independence.

7. Eliminate one money-draining habit

Alright, so maybe you're not ready to give up your entire lifestyle yet. In that case, start with one hobby or habit that costs you money every month. If you can't think of anything, check your most recent bank statement and highlight the deductions that went to wants, not needs. If you go to the movies a couple of times every month, stop going and stream your movies instead. If you enjoy purchasing stuff on Amazon every few weeks, stop doing it and replace it with a cheaper alternative like going to the library every few weeks. Once you've successfully eliminated a habit, you can continue you with your other money-wasting habits.

8.   Push your mental boundaries

Our biggest limitations are our minds. Begin by working backward with your budget, cut your expenses down and boost your income. With discipline and creativity, it's possible to live on half your income. All it takes is your determination and perseverance.

Get the information you need to start investing

Do you want to invest but have no idea where to start? The first step to investing is the most important. If you invest wisely, it can lead to financial independence and passive income.

If you want to start investing, you need to have the right information so you avoid wasting your money on poor investments. So, what information should you have to get started? Here is what you need to know to ensure your investment is a success:

1.   Decide on the type of assets you want to own

Investing is about putting money in something today and getting more money out of it in the future. Usually, you can achieve that by acquiring productive assets. For instance, if you buy an apartment building, you will own the property and the cash that it produces through rent.

Each productive asset has unique characteristics as well as pros and cons. Here are some of the potential investments you might consider:

Business equity – Owning equity in a business enables you to share a profit or loss generated by the company. Whether you want to own that equity by buying shares of a publicly traded business or acquiring a small business outright, business equities are the most rewarding asset class.

Fixed income securities - When you decide to invest in fixed income security, you are lending money to a bond issuer. In exchange, you will get an interest income. You can do so in many ways: from US saving bonds to tax-free municipal bonds, from corporate bonds to money markets and certificates of deposit.

Real estate – Real estate is perhaps the most easily understood and oldest asset class investors. You can make money by investing in real estate in several ways, but it comes down to either owning something and letting others use it for lease payments or rent, or developing property and selling it for profit.

Intangible property and rights – Intangible property consist of everything from patents and trademarks to copyrights and music royalties.

Farmland and other commodity-producing goods – investment in commodity-producing activities involve extracting or producing something from nature or the ground. It usually involves improving it and selling it to make a profit. If there is oil on your land, you can extract it and get cash. If you grow corn, you can sell it and make money. It can involve a lot of risks – disasters, weather, and other challenges that might make you lose money – but you can still make money from it.

2.   Decide how you want to own these assets

When you have decided on the assets you want to own, you can decide how you to own them. To understand this point, let's look at business equity. Let's say you want a stake in a publicly traded business. Will you go for shares outright or will you go through a pooled structure?

- **Outright ownership** – This way, you will directly buy shares from an individual company and you will see them in your balance sheet or that of the entity you own. You will be an actual share shareholder and have voting rights. It might give you access to dividend income. Your net worth might rise as the company grows.

- **Pooled ownership** – With this method, you will add your money to a pool contributed to by other people and buy ownership through a shared entity or structure. Most of the time, this is done through mutual funds. If you are a wealthy investor, you can invest in hedge funds. If you don't have a large amount of money, you can consider investing index funds and exchange-traded funds.

3. Decide where you want to hold the assets

When you have made up your mind on how you want to acquire investment assets, you need to decide how you want to hold these assets. There are several options:

• **Taxable account** – If you decide on taxable accounts like a brokerage account, you will pay tax later but there won't be any restrictions on your money. You will be free to spend it on anything you want. You will be free to cash in and buy anything you want. You can also add any amount you want to it every year.

• **Tax shelters** - If you choose to invest in things like Roth IRA or 401(k) plan, there are tax and asset protection benefits. Some retirement plans and accounts offer unlimited bankruptcy protection. This means that should a medical disaster strike that wipes out your balance sheet, the creditors won't touch your investment capital. Some are tax-deferred. This means you might get tax deductions when you deposit the capital into an account to choose investment and pay taxes in the future. Good tax planning can mean massive extra wealth in the future.

• **Trust other asset protection mechanisms** – You can hold your investments through structures or entities like trust funds. You will get major asset protection and planning benefits when you use these special ownership methods. This is useful when you want to restrict how your capital is used. Also, if you have significant real estate investments or operating assets, you can speak to your attorney to set up a holding company.

The information you need to start building your personal assets

There are a lot of ways to build personal assets with little money, but few people know how to do it. What could be the problem? The problem is most people don't know about the important process of asset building.

What should one do to build assets? It's not rocket science. If you learn the process of asset building, the rest is easy.

Invest money to accumulate assets

You should know all about the relationship between asset accumulation and investments.

• **Investments** – Investing is the process of buying assets. Investments are generally made in either stocks, bonds, or cash equivalents. Investments are made with the intention of generating income and earning profits over time. When investments succeed, they are a great way to make passive income. In other words, money gets made without the need for daily upkeep.

• **Asset accumulation** – When you gradually acquire assets over time and hold it for the long term, assets will start to accumulate. These assets consist of your earnings, savings, and the returns on your investments.

• **Asset building** – Asset building is the process of gradually buying assets or acquiring resources with the intention of accumulation. This practice can help families achieve stability, create good credit, save for the future, and ultimately strengthen their communities.

When you buy assets without the intention of accumulation, it becomes a meaningless activity. Without them, it is much more difficult to save for the future.

Since you now understand the process of asset building, let's ask a more basic question.

Why build assets?

If you're interested in achieving financial independence, then you'll want to consider building assets. Why is that necessary?

Do you love your job? I know few people who would raise their hands to that question. If most people don't love their jobs, why do they keep them? It's simple: we need the money so we feel we don't have another choice. It all comes down to the basic need for survival. We think our jobs are inextricably linked to this.

We must compromise to do our jobs because we want to continue earning income. Is there a way to remove this dependency? You may not believe this, but it's absolutely possible. All you have to do is make the necessary changes to your lifestyle and spending habits to achieve financial independence. It's much easier than you think. Here is an approach to help you.

• Realize that you depend on your job for income and understand that there is an alternative. Most people who work don't realize that financial independence exists.

• Start eliminating financial dependence gradually. You can do this by generating an alternative source of income. Where will your alternative source of income come from? From investing in assets. Consider which assets will add the biggest value to your life.

How can a common man build assets?

For those who are already affluent, asset building methods are different. How can a common man build assets? Here are the steps:

1. **Save** – Saving money is very important. The easiest way one can save money is by putting aside some of their income. Eliminating unnecessary spending will increase cash-in-hand. Even millionaires must save money if they want to stay rich. If you save above 25% of your total income, that is considered a decent saving. You can make an automatic transfer where 25% of your money goes automatically to your savings account.

Saving money also allows you to have more money to invest with. When you make larger investments, you can expect bigger returns when the money multiplies.

Here are some other ideas to help you keep more money in your bank account.

- **Build an emergency fund** – Nothing eats assets faster than an emergency. When something unexpected happens, it can consume a lot of money. An example is a medical emergency. It's recommended that you keep sufficient back-up to handle emergencies. Consider saving for an emergency in cash and insurance.
- **Arrange a recurring deposit** – The priority here is to save. You shouldn't think about a return. There are some advantages to recurring deposits. Savings will be automatic, money is safe, and money remains in the bank.
  Building an emergency fund ensures that we are prepared to meet life's emergencies. When they happen, we can depend on our savings. Arranging for recurring deposits ensures that what we save can be used for investments.

2. Invest – Why do you need to invest and not keep building savings to buy assets directly? It would be nice to do that, but holding your money as savings isn't recommended. That's because savings can easily be spent. And don't forget, investing your money makes it multiply.

When you have gone through all the effort of saving, you should ensure that you invest that money wisely. Most people have no idea how. Here are some examples of different investments you can make. Many investment experts even advise utilizing more than one method.

- Hybrid funds – Hybrid funds have a SIP, which is a useful tool for investments. There are several benefits. You will get exposure to debt and equity from one window. You should develop a mindset to keep you investing in this fund through

SIPs. Keep doing this month after month without stopping.

- Index ETFs – ETFs, also known as Exchange-Traded Funds, can make a worthwhile investment and can encompass many types of investments, such as bonds, stocks, and other types. ETFs offers great investment diversification within an equity portfolio. You can get ETF units every time there is above a 3% dip in an index.
- Gold – Gold can be a long-term investment that takes up to 12 years. Unlike the other forms of investments, you can actually hold this investment in your own hands.
- Buy land – Land is an asset that has become scarce. It's a great idea to invest in land on the outskirts of a city, though all investments in land can be risky. This is because it doesn't produce an income unless you do something with it, and in the meantime, it can cost you a lot in taxes. If you're considering investing in land, make sure you have a plan, and it may be wise to talk to an expert.
- Trade Cryptocurrencies – This method of investing is not devoid of its risks, but many people insist there's a lot more money to be made in cryptocurrency investments. In recent years, many bitcoin investors have made fortunes, though many have also lost. Cryptocurrencies can bring you big rewards when invested in wisely. We advise educating yourself before purchasing any.

3. **Locked funds** – This step is very important. Most people would stop at step two. In this step, you will be converting all your assets into income generating assets. How can this be done? You can consider REITs, rental properties, and dividend-paying stocks.

Since the above steps are very crucial to asset building, let's go into more detail on how we can implement them successfully.

The money you locked in land, SIP, and RD has only one objective. You can redeem it and use it to buy assets at some point. You can use it on income generating assets. Consider the following:

- **Dividend-paying stocks** – These are strong stocks which pay regular dividends to the shareholder. You should buy these stocks at the right price. If you fail to do so, its yield will be too low. You should wait for a perfect time to get the best dividend paying stocks.
- **Rental property** – This might be the best income generating asset you can get, as it generates the best passive income and depending on the property, this passive income can be a sizable sum. What you earn from real estate property also increases the rate of inflation.

You should consider distributing your investments among the above options. These are perfect investment vehicles for income generation.

What's the difference between trading and investing?

Both trading and investing involve making a profit by buying and selling stocks. What sets them apart, however, is how they go about achieving those goals. Trading is more concerned with using the stock market for short-term gains, while investments are usually a long-term commitment that takes place over years and sometimes even decades.

Trading involves higher risks than investing, but also higher returns. This is because stock prices can fluctuate a lot within a short period of time. Timing is, in fact, a major factor that needs to be considered, in the world of trading.

Investing is significantly lower in risk, but don't expect any big returns right away. Investments can get you big rewards, but these will take some time.

How to make successful investments and get big rewards

Now that you're no longer relying on material goods, you likely have more money to spare for your investments. You may even be interested in stocks. Although it may seem simple at first glance, there's a lot more to trading and investing than simply making a purchase and waiting for the dough to roll in. For the most fruitful outcome, you must stay informed on a variety of different factors.

When it comes to buying stocks, it's not enough to just make any investment or trade. In fact, investing in the wrong thing could result in a major loss. To win big from an investment, you need to make calculated efforts in the right direction. You must consider all your options carefully and resist the urge to throw your money at absolutely anything. To ensure that both your trades and investments are successful, keep these useful tips in mind.

1. Don't just fall for the idea

Let's face it, in this day and age, everyone has a good idea. And as for the great ideas out there, chances are that someone has had the same one before. For this reason, you shouldn't throw your money at just any good idea. Take other factors into account. Which company is in charge of this good idea? What is their business plan? There are many reasons why a good idea could lead to a loss or nothing at all. Instead of falling for the idea, fall for the company instead.

2. Always do the research

You may get a good feeling right from the get-go, but good feelings can be wrong. Don't let your financial future suffer for it. Traders should always do their research. Not just into various companies, but also trading patterns and other trends. Resist the urge to wing it and stay completely informed on the entire trading landscape. Understand that everything can affect what happens to your hard-earned money.

3. Spread out your investments

A good tip for avoiding huge losses is to make sure you don't invest in solely one company. Instead, try spreading out your investments between a few different options. Learn from the old saying, "Don't keep all your eggs in one basket." It rings particularly true for investing. This way, if any loss occurs, it won't be catastrophic and you'll still have stocks in other companies. If disaster strikes a company you've invested in, you won't make a huge loss. It may seem unlikely for this to happen, but this is exactly the type of attitude that can lead to losses from carelessness. Many investors have lost billions by failing to take this precaution. For example, in the Enron company scandal.

4. Take some risks

Studies have shown that the crushing disappointment we feel when we lose money is greater than the joy we feel when we win. To avoid these negative feelings, many investors and traders avoid making any risks at all in their pursuits. While we don't advise making big risks all the time, it can pay off to take a leap every now and then. Sometimes you can get very lucky. Just make sure that, should a loss occur, it won't affect your financial standing in a significant way. Make smart risks and you just might find yourself making big returns.

5. Don't overestimate your abilities

After all the time and effort spent staring at the screen, you've finally made a return. Congrats! While this is definitely something to celebrate, don't let your winners' high cloud your judgment. You're not invincible and you could easily lose it all if you don't continue to be careful. Rewards don't always indicate the skill of a trader, sometimes it can all be down to luck. Don't take any wild risks on an impulse. Always invest wisely.

Remember to try and enjoy the world of investing. While it's true that there are many risky aspects to it, it'll bring you more satisfaction and control than putting that same money in needless items. To truly honor the minimalist philosophy, only invest in what you really believe in, and resist the urge to invest in everything.

Greater life satisfaction will come when you take control of your finances back from every whim, fleeting desire and impulse. This is the minimalist way.

Conclusion

Thank you for making it to the end of the Minimalist Budget Mindset.

Let's hope it was informative and able to provide you with all the information you need to manage your money well and achieve your financial goals. With more tools in your money-saving arsenal, you'll find it much easier to take those strides towards financial freedom.

You have learned that minimalism can put an end to the gluttony of the world that surrounds us. It's the opposite of what you see in advertisements on TV. We live in a society that prides itself on buying a lot of needless products; we are overwhelmed by consumerist habits, clutter, material possessions, debt, noise, and distractions. What we don't seem to have enough of, however, is true meaning in our lives and intentionality in our actions. With all you've learned, you'll find it much easier to shut out the noisy consumerist world, with its many money-grabbing ploys.

Adopting a minimalist lifestyle will allow you to eliminate the things you don't need so you can concentrate on what really completes your life. Once you start shifting your values, the money-saving techniques we've demonstrated we'll feel like second nature.

You have learned exactly how you can save money as a minimalist. Saving money this way has a lot of benefits and it could save you a lot of distress in the future. You have learned how to track your spending and how you can start saving money. This has taught you how to be disciplined when money is involved.

Other than that, you have learned some of the best budgeting strategies to help you achieve your goals. Apply these strategies as soon as you can to achieve financial goals sooner than you expect. Don't feel daunted, as you may find them easier than you think.

Getting out of debt has never been easy for most of us, but learning about the causes of debt has helped you view debt differently and learn effective ways to get out of it. These methods will help you get out of debt while at the same time helping you save more.

When you have eliminated debt and learned how to save, consider investing in something that will multiply your money. With the information you have learned about investing, and the life-altering self-discipline you have gained, you will view investing from a different angle and start accumulating personal wealth. Use your newly discovered tips wisely to ensure you minimize any potential losses and make more frequent gains.

You've now learned how to develop a minimalist mindset and make the big savings that all successful minimalists do. Practice makes perfect, and that's what you need to do with your new minimalist budget mindset. With some time and practice, you will be able to make use of good money habits and make it your part of life.